eclipse |

the Gift

by Janice Okoh

The Gift was first produced as a co-production between
Eclipse Theatre and Belgrade Theatre Coventry. It premiered
in Coventry on Saturday 18 January 2020 followed by
a UK tour visiting six cities.

FOREWORD

Revolution Mix, the Eclipse movement from 2015 onwards, has worked with a group of writers researching five centuries of an untapped vein of British history. This was the jumping-off point for our aim to produce the largest ever body of new Black British work in Theatre, Film and Radio.

The first production – *Black Men Walking* – was an epic walk across the Peaks that uncovered 2,000 years of hidden Black Yorkshire histories. Inspired by a real walking group, it had a sold-out UK tour.

The Last Flag (BBC Radio 4 Afternoon Play) is set in an imagined near-future world where identity and empathy are electronically controlled.

Princess & The Hustler was a more recent but equally forgotten story from Bristol. This 1963 story was a domestic drama set in the home of a Black family that cleverly combined the politics of colourism with The Bristol Bus Boycott – a seminal Black British civil rights action that led to the Race Relations Act of 1965. *Princess & The Hustler* is a story of Black agency that is funny, powerful and uplifting.

As the new Artistic Director and CEO of Eclipse, I have the privilege of introducing you to this extraordinary play by Janice Okoh. On first reading, I couldn't wait to join together with you our audiences and take in what our cast and crew have created from this groundbreaking new play directed by the inimitable Dawn Walton.

Amanda Huxtable
Artistic Director and CEO, Eclipse

the Gift

by Janice Okoh

CAST

Aggie / Sarah	Donna Berlin
Harriet Waller / Queen Victoria	Joanna Brookes
Mrs Schoen / Harriet	Rebecca Charles
James / James Davies	Dave Fishley
Sarah Bonetta Davies	Shannon Hayes
Ben / Reverend Venn	Richard Teverson

CREATIVE TEAM

Director	Dawn Walton
Designer	Simon Kenny
Lighting Designer	Johanna Town
Composer & Sound Designer	Adrienne Quartly
Movement Director & Associate Director	Vicki Igbokwe
Casting Director	Briony Barnett
Dramaturg	Ola Animashawun
Voice & Dialect Coach	Hazel Holder
Etiquette Coach	Louise Kempton
Fight Director	Stephen Medlin

For this production

Executive Producer	Peter Huntley for Smart Entertainment
Tour Production Manager	James Anderton
Production Manager	Adrian Sweeney for Belgrade Theatre
Company Stage Manager	Anna-Lisa Maree
Deputy Stage Manger	Shannon Martin
Assistant Stage Manager	Sophie Keers
Head of Wigs & Wardrobe	Elizabeth Greengrass
Wig Supervisor	Sid Kennedy
Production Carpenter	Robert Oatley
LX Programmer	Francis James
Observing Director	Jet Sebbie Mudhai

CAST

DONNA BERLIN | AGGIE / SARAH

Theatre credits include: *Chasing Rainbows* (Hoxton Hall); *Princess & The Hustler* (Eclipse Theatre – nominated for 'Best Supporting Actress', Broadway World Regional 2019 Awards); *A Midsummer Night's Dream* (Crucible); *The Chalk Garden* (Chichester Festival Theatre); *Great Apes* (Arcola); *Of Kith and Kin* (Crucible, Bush); *Anna Karenina* and *Rolling Stone* (Royal Exchange, Leeds Playhouse); *Blood Wedding* and *The Bacchae* (Royal & Derngate, Northampton); *Keeping Mum* (Brockley Jack); *Counted* and *Look Right, Look Left* (County Hall); *Puffins* (Nabokov, Southwark Playhouse) and *The Vagina Monologues* (Pleasance). Television credits include: *Requiem; Game Face; EastEnders; Todd Margaret; Drifters; Coronation Street; Hollyoaks; New Tricks; Extras – Series B; Lead Balloon; Casualty; Doctors; Judge John Deed* and *Beautiful People.* Film credits include: *In Darkness; Monochrome; Dinner With My Sisters; Press Your Lips* (short) and *Blinda* (short).

JOANNA BROOKES | HARRIET WALLER / QUEEN VICTORIA

Theatre credits include: *Pride and Prejudice* (Theatre Royal Bury St Edmunds); *Witness For The Prosecution* (County Hall); *Much Ado About Nothing* and *The Daughter in Law* (Watford Palace); *Spider's Web* (The Mill); *Monster Raving Loony* (Theatre Royal Plymouth, Soho); *The Rise and Fall of Little Voice* (Leeds Playhouse, Birmingham Rep); *The Importance of Being Earnest* (Nottingham Playhouse); *The Physicists* (Donmar Warehouse); *The Rivals, Spring and Port Wine* and *The Admirable Crichton* (New Vic); *The Biggleswades* (Southwark Playhouse); *The Waltz of The Toreadors* (Chichester Festival Theatre) and *Romeo and Juliet* (Exeter Northcott). Television credits include: *Cheat; The Windsors Royal Wedding Special; Coronation Street; Man Down; We The Jury; Uncle; The Tunnel; Mr Selfridge; Law and Order; Boomers; Siblings; Doctors; Holby City; Taking The Flak; Phoneshop; Dancing on the Edge; Mrs Biggs; Bad Girls; Fifteen Storeys High; Jonathan Creek; The Inspector Lynley Mysteries; Sir Gadabout; Titmuss Regained* and *Survival of The Fittest.* Radio credits include: *Ed Reardon's Week; The Exorcist; Votes For Women; The Archers; Mr Bridger's Orphan; Up The Junction; Georgy Girl; The Author of Himself; When the Dog Dies; My Blue Heaven; Me and Joe; Weekending; A Square of One's Own; House of The Spirit Levels; Kate and Cindy; Do Nothing Till You Hear From Me; Nigel; Earl and Sort Out the World; Rent; Harry Hill's Fruit Corner; Double Income No Kids Yet* and *Three Off The Tee.* Film credits include: *Rocks; Their Finest; Film Stars Don't Die in Liverpool; Criminal; Pauline* and *Kid.*

REBECCA CHARLES | MRS SCHOEN / HARRIET
Theatre credits include: *Abigail's Party* (Hull Truck); *An Ideal Husband* (Vaudeville); *The Graduate* and *Wicked Old Man* (Leeds Playhouse); *The Father* (Wyndham's, Duke of York, Tricycle, Theatre Royal Bath); *Les Liaisons Dangereuses, Just Between Ourselves* and *The Norman Conquests* (Salisbury Playhouse); *The Old Country* (English Touring Theatre, Trafalgar Studios); *Julius Caesar* (Barbican); *Great Expectations* (Royal Exchange); *Boston Marriage* (Bolton Octagon); *Uncle Vanya* (The Wrestling School, Hebble Theatre Berlin); *Richard III* and *The Importance of Being Earnest* (Derby Playhouse); *The Castle* (The Wrestling School); *Hated Nightfall* (Royal Court); *The Recruiting Officer* and *A Midsummer Night's Dream* (Royal Lyceum); *Cyrano de Bergerac* (Haymarket); *Blithe Spirit* (Harrogate); *Peter Pan* (Theatr Clwyd); *Boston Story* (The Mill at Sonning); *A Pin to See the Peepshow* (Redgrave); *Mrs Dot* (Watford Palace). Television credits include: *We Hunt Together; Casualty; EastEnders; Homefront; Doctors; Midsomer Murders; Heartbeat; The Office; Hear the Silence; Foyle's War; People Like Us; The Bill; The Peter Principle; Jonathan Creek; Over Here; Jewels; The House of Eliott* and *Fatal Inversion*. Film credits include: *The Heart of Me; Bridget Jones's Diary; Shakespeare in Love* and *Mrs Brown*. Radio credits include: *The Father*.

DAVE FISHLEY | JAMES / JAMES DAVIES
Theatre credits include: *Our Country's Good* (Nottingham Playhouse, Ramps on the Moon); *Queen Anne* (Royal Shakespeare Company, Theatre Royal Haymarket); *Macbeth* (Theatre Severn); *Treasure Island* and *Of Mice and Men* (Birmingham Rep); *Hamlet, As You Like It* and *All's Well That Ends Well* (Royal Shakespeare Company); *The Taming of the Shrew* (Southwark Playhouse); *Rough Crossings* (Headlong); *The Odyssey* (Lyric Hammersmith, Bristol Old Vic); *Macbeth* (Out of Joint); *Paradise Lost* (Bristol Old Vic); *A Special Relationship* (York Theatre Royal); *Dido, Queen of Carthage* (Shakespeare's Globe); *Crime and Punishment in Dalston* (Arcola); *Caledonian Road* (Almeida); *The Nativity* (Young Vic); *Twelfth Night* (Nuffield Southampton); *Eritrea – The Other War* (Leeds Playhouse); *Marat/Sade* (National Theatre); *Silver face* (Notting Hill Gate); *Now You Know* (Hampstead); *Asylum! Asylum!* (Crowley Peacock, Abbey); *Smoke* (Royal Exchange) and *The Tempest* and *Macbeth* (English Shakespeare Company). Television credits include: *Moses Jones; See How They Run; Casualty; Buried; Judge John Deed; The Bill; Touch of Frost; Macbeth* and *Between the Lines*. Film credits include: *Bridget Jones's Diary; If Only; The Fifth Element; Solitaire for Two* and *The Gathering*.

SHANNON HAYES | SARAH BONETTA DAVIES
Theatre credits include: *Constellations* (Oxford University Drama Society, Experimental Theatre Club); *As We Forgive Those* (Oxford University Drama Society); *4.48 Psychosis* and *Other Hands* (Oxford University Drama Society, Identity) and *His Dark Materials Part 2* (Peculiar Spectacles).Television credits include: *Years and Years; Cold Feet; Kiss Me First; Vera; Ted Lasso* and *Undercover*. Film credits include: *Totally Maisy; What You Gonna Do?; Locked* and *Tyger Tyger*.

RICHARD TEVERSON | BEN / REVEREND VENN

Theatre credits include: *Richard III* and *Romeo and Juliet* (Shakespeare's Rose York); *The Libertine* (Theatre Royal Haymarket, Theatre Royal Bath); *Private Lives* (UK tour); *Handbagged* (UK tour); *How Many Miles To Babylon* (Lyric Belfast); *The Schoolmistress* (Stephen Joseph); *The Winslow Boy* and *Cause Célèbre* (Old Vic); *Somersaults* (Finborough); *The Doctor's Dilemma* and *After the Dance* (National Theatre); *The 39 Steps* (Criterion); *When Harry Met Sally* and *A Woman of No Importance* (Theatre Royal Haymarket); *The Lion King* (Lyceum); *Private Lives, Tons of Money* and *Hobson's Choice* (Freud Company); *The Singing Group* (Chelsea); *Cleo, Camping, Emmanuelle & Dick* (New Vic) and *A Midsummer Night's Dream* (Creation). Television credits include: *The Crown*; *Whiskey Cavalier*; *Call the Midwife*; *Taboo*; *Downton Abbey*; *Coalition*; *Jamaica Inn*; *The Bletchley Circle*; *Spies of Warsaw*; *Dancing on the Edge*; *Upstairs Downstairs*; *The Roman Mysteries*; *Live! Girls! Dogtown*; *Balderdash & Piffle*; *Poirot-Five Little Pigs* and *The Project*. Film credits include: *Red Joan*; *The Mercy*; *Private Peaceful*; *Brideshead Revisited* and *Workhorse*.

CREATIVE TEAM

JANICE OKOH | WRITER

Janice Okoh is an award-winning playwright. Her first play *Egusi Soup* was produced in 2012 and went on a national tour in 2014. It won a Channel 4 Playwriting Award in 2017. Her second play *Three Birds* won the Bruntwood Playwriting Prize in 2011 and was shortlisted for the Verity Bargate and Alfred Fagon Awards in that same year. Janice has recently completed a 30-minute drama for Channel 4's diversity scheme, *4 Stories*. Janice has written for television and is an established radio dramatist.

DAWN WALTON | DIRECTOR

Dawn Walton is a director of theatre, film and radio whose recent theatre productions include: *Red Dust Road* (National Theatre of Scotland); *salt.* (Selina Thompson Productions). For Eclipse Theatre: *Princess & The Hustler*, *Black Men Walking*, *A Raisin in the Sun*, *One Monkey Don't Stop No Show* and *The Hounding of David Oluwale*. For Royal Court Theatre: *Oxford Street*, *93.2fm*. For Young Vic Theatre: *Winners*; *The Blacks* and *Lyrikal Fearta* (Sadler's Wells) and has received nominations for Olivier Awards and at the UK Theatre Awards. In 2009, Dawn founded Eclipse Theatre and for ten years was Artistic Director and CEO of the company, creating two major movements; 'Revolution Mix' which is delivering the largest ever national delivery of new Black British productions in theatre, film and radio and 'Slate: Black. Arts. World', supporting over 2,000 Black artists in the North.

SIMON KENNY | DESIGNER

Previous designs for Eclipse include *Black Men Walking* and *Princess & The Hustler*. The design for *Black Men Walking* was recently selected to represent the UK at the 2019 Prague Quadrennial of Performance Design and at the V&A Museum. Theatre credits include: *Ghost Quartet* (Boulevard); *Assassins* (Watermill, Nottingham Playhouse); *Red Dust Road* (National Theatre of Scotland); *Noughts & Crosses* (Pilot); the multi award-winning *Sweeney Todd* in a purpose built pie shop (West End, Off-Broadway); *The Children* (English Theatre Frankfurt); *Cabaret* (Deutsches Theater Munich); *The Selfish Giant*, a new folk opera by Guy Chambers (Vaudeville); *Macbeth* (Stafford Castle); *Holes* (Nottingham Playhouse); *Broken Glass* (Watford Palace); *Babette's Feast* (Print Room); *In the Next Room or the vibrator play* (Ustinov); *Island* (National Theatre); *Twelfth Night* and *The Merchant of Venice* (Shakespeare's Globe). Opera credits include: *A Midsummer Night's Dream* and *Le nozze di Figaro* (Nevill Holt); *Vivienne* (Royal Opera House Linbury); *The Cunning Little Vixen*, *Háry János* and *Orlando* (Ryedale Festival).

JOHANNA TOWN | LIGHTING DESIGNER

Johanna is an Associate Artist for Theatre503, the Chair of the Association of Lighting Designers, and a Fellow of Guildhall School of Music and Drama. Theatre credits include: *Two Ladies* (Bridge); *The Butterfly Lion, The Watsons, The Norman Conquests, Fracked* and *Educating Rita* (Chichester Festival); *Some Like It Hip Hop* (tour); *Queen Margaret, Frankenstein, Guys and Dolls* and *The House of Bernarda Alba* (Royal Exchange); *Rutherford and Son, Love and Information, One Flew Over the Cuckoo's Nest* (Crucible, Sheffield); *Don Quixote* (Royal Shakespeare Company); *Brainstorming, Moon on a Rainbow Shawl* and *The Permanent Way* (National Theatre); *Blithe Spirit, The Crucible* (Pitlochry Festival); *Creditors/Miss Julie, Jeeves and Wooster in Perfect Nonsense* and *Sense & Sensibility* (Theatre by the Lake); *Napoli Brooklyn* (Original Theatre); *Her Naked Skin* and *The Magna Carta Plays* (Salisbury Playhouse); *Shook* and *Trestle* (Southwark Playhouse); *The Big Corner* and *The Tenant of Wildfell Hall* (Octagon, Bolton); *Botticelli in the Fire, Experience, Deposit* and *Describe The Night* (Hampstead); *What the Butler Saw, Fences, Dear Lupin, Betrayal, Via Dolorosa* and *Beautiful Thing* (West End); *My Name is Rachel Corrie, Rose, Guantanamo, Our Lady of Sligo, Haunted, Arabian Nights* and *The Steward of Christendom* (New York).

ADRIENNE QUARTLY | COMPOSER & SOUND DESIGNER

Adrienne is a sound designer and composer for theatre. Theatre credits include: *The Girl Who Fell* (Trafalgar Studios); *Citysong* (Abbey, Dublin, Soho); *Queen Margaret* (Royal Exchange); *The Paper Man* (Improbable); *Kindertransport* and *The Crucible* (Les Théâtres de la Ville de Luxembourg); *Get Happy* (Beijing Comedy Festival); *Opening Skinners Box* (Lincoln Centre Festival, NYC); *A Tale of Two Cities* (Royal & Derngate, Northampton); *Bad Jews* (Theatre Royal Haymarket); *I am Thomas* (Told by an Idiot, National Theatre of Scotland); *Splendour* (Donmar Warehouse); *The Ghost Train* (Told by an Idiot); *Inside Wagner's Head* (Royal Opera House); *Frauline Julie (*Schaubühne, Berlin, Barbican); *Stockholm* (Frantic Assembly); *Rings of Saturn* (Halle Kalk, Cologne) and *Thomas Hobbes* (Royal Shakespeare Company). Adrienne was part of the team on the Olivier nominated *Cuttin' It* (Young Vic); *Black Men Walking* (Eclipse – Best New Play nomination, UK Theatre Awards) and *Rose* (HOME – Best Production, Manchester Theatre Awards)

VICKI IGBOKWE | MOVEMENT DIRECTOR & ASSOCIATE DIRECTOR
Vicki is a choreographer, movement director and founder of Uchenna, a dance company based in London. Dance credits include: *Our Mighty Groove* and *The Head Wrap Diaries* (Uchenna); *Hansel & Gretel* (Uchenna, The Place) and *Fierce & Free* (Uchenna, Sadler's Wells, The Lowry, Birmingham Hippodrome). Theatre credits include: *Provok'd* (Guildhall, Barbican); *The Woods* and *A Kind of People* (Royal Court); *Princess & The Hustler* (Eclipse Theatre); *Little Bevan* (Pentabus); *Mid Life* (Diverse City); *Seven Ages of Patience – A Friendly Society* (Kiln) and *Red Dust Road* (National Theatre of Scotland). Film credits include: *Bohemian Rhapsody*. Television credits include: *London 2012*; *Sochi 2014*; *Glasgow 2014* and *Azerbaijan Islamic Solidarity Games 2017*.

BRIONY BARNETT | CASTING DIRECTOR
Briony has worked in casting for over ten years in theatre, film and television. Theatre credits include: *Again* (West End); *The Trick* and *An Adventure* (Bush); *Abigail's Party* (Hull Truck); *Black Men Walking, A Raisin in the Sun* and *One Monkey Don't Stop No Show* (Eclipse Theatre); *Female Parts* and *Chasing Rainbows* (Hoxton Hall); *Fences* (Theatre Royal Bath); *Ticking* (Trafalgar Studios); *Play Mas* (Orange Tree); *Boy with Beer* (King's Head); *Chiaroscuro* (Bush); *When The Crows Visit* and *Half God of Rainfall* (Kiln) and *The Invisible Hand, Ben Hur, A Wolf in Snakeskin Shoes, The House That Will Not Stand, The Colby Sisters, Detaining Justice, Seize the Day, Handbagged, White Teeth* and *Not Black and White* (Tricycle). Film credits include: *Bruce; Gypsy's Kiss; The Knot; What We Did On Our Holiday; Common People; Tezz; Final Prayer; Stop; Love/Loss; Zero Sum; Travellers; Janet and Bernard; The Knot; A Sunny Morning; Tezz; Value Life; Frequency* and *Our Time Alone; Conversation Piece; Tears of the Son; Jhoom Barabar Jhoom; Love Aajkal; Jhootha Sahi; Red Tails; The Walker* and, for Eclipse Theatre, *Samuel's Trousers* and *10by10*. Television credits include: *Outnumbered; Just Around the Corner; Inside the Mind of Leonardo; The Fixer; Generation Kill; Five Days; Tsunami the Aftermath; Kingdom*.

OLA ANIMASHAWUN | DRAMATURG

Ola Animashawun is the National Theatre Connections Dramaturg and the Co-Founder and Creative Director of the playwriting consultancy, Euphoric Ink. He is also a former Associate Director of the Royal Court Theatre, where he worked for 23 years, during which time he founded and ran the Royal Court Young Writers Programme, and set up a nationwide writers' programme, dedicated to finding and nurturing new African, Caribbean, Asian and other ethnic minority playwrights – Critical Mass. Ola has worked in theatre for over 30 years, with 20 of those years dedicated to specialising in script development as a dramaturg and facilitator. He is an Associate Artist, Dramaturg and Mentor for Belgrade Theatre Coventry, Theatre Absolute, Shop Front Theatre, and Eclipse Theatre. His other skills include, acting, directing, devising and writing. He is also a patron of Graeae Theatre and Script Yorkshire and an Honorary Fellow of the Royal Central School of Speech and Drama.

HAZEL HOLDER | VOICE & DIALECT COACH

Theatre credits includes: *Black Men Walking* (Eclipse Theatre); *Nine Night, Pericles, Barber Shop Chronicles, Angels in America, Les Blancs* and *Ma Rainey's Black Bottom* (National Theatre); *Tina: The Tina Turner Musical* (Aldwych); *Caroline, or Change* (Playhouse, Chichester Festival); *Death of a Salesman, The Convert, The Mountaintop, The Emperor* and *Cuttin' It* (Young Vic); *Ear for Eye, Poet in Da Corner, Grimly Handsome, Pigs and Dogs* and *Father Comes Home from the Wars* (Royal Court); *Richard II* (Sam Wanamaker Playhouse); *Our Lady of Kibeho* (Royal & Derngate, Northampton); *Death of a Salesman* and *Guys and Dolls* (Royal Exchange); *Leave Taking* (Bush); *Little Shop of Horrors* (Regent's Park Open Air Theatre); *Twilight: LA – 1992* and *Eclipsed* (Gate); *Half Breed* and *Girls* (Talawa, Soho). Television credits include: *Victoria; In The Long Run; Poldark; No Offence* and *Broken*. Film credits include: *Small Axe; Death on the Nile; War of the Worlds* and *Hanna 2*.

PETER HUNTLEY FOR SMART ENTERTAINMENT | EXECUTIVE PRODUCER

Smart Entertainment was founded by Peter Huntley in 2017 following a decade working with some of the UK's leading producers. Peter was Associate Producer of *Bend It Like Beckham* at the Phoenix and General Manager of *The Wind in the Willows* on UK tour and at the London Palladium. He was Executive Producer of a cinema release of *The Wind in the Willows*. Recent productions include: *Black Men Walking* (Eclipse Theatre); *Our Lady of Kibeho, The Pope* and *The Lovely Bones* (Royal & Derngate, Northampton); *Bullet Tongue Reloaded* (The Big House); *The Wipers Times* (Arts, UK tour); *Trial by Laughter* (UK tour); *It Happened in Key West* (Charing Cross); and concerts of *A Night at the Musicals* (UK tour); *A Christmas Carol* (Lyceum); *Camelot* (Palladium) and *Girlfriends* (Bishopsgate Institute).

STEPHEN MEDLIN | FIGHT DIRECTOR

Steve Medlin trained at Rose Bruford Drama School and with a variety of physical theatre companies and artists including David Glass, Adrian Hedley and Theatre de Complicité and is a founder member of Unclassified Arts. Steve is a specialist in physical theatre and a regular actor and trainer with BBC Academy. He has appeared in television and film productions such as *Sweeney Todd*, *Jungle Run*, *Pump It Up*, *The Nutcracker*, *M.O.T.H*, *Amar, Acbar & Tony* and *Sticks and Stones*. He has worked as a movement specialist for a wide variety of theatres and companies both nationally and internationally across the last 30 years. He has been Movement Director on a number of Eclipse shows including *Black Men Walking*, *The Hounding of David Oluwale*, *There's Only One Wayne Mathews*, *One Monkey Don't Stop No Show* and *A Raisin in the Sun* as well as Eclipse's set of 10by10 films and new short *Samuel's Trousers* (currently in post-production). He has devised and directed new productions *Journeys Beyond*, co-produced by Eclipse as well as *Grimm Tales*, *7ages* and *Fable* with Wac Arts. He is one of the originators and current course leader of the innovative training programme at Wac Arts that gives equal status to non-western art forms as well as the Artistic Director of Collage Voices in Wood Green.

eclipse | **REVO LUTION MIX**

ECLIPSE TEAM

Artistic Director and CEO   Amanda Huxtable
Executive Producer   Shawab Iqbal
General Manager   Jonathan Ennis
Marketing Manager   Kelly France
Audience Development Producer   Yinka Ayinde

Find out more
eclipsetheatre.org.uk
/eclipsetcl #TheGift

THE GIFT

Janice Okoh

Just like moons and like suns,
With the certainty of tides,
Just like hopes springing high,
Still I rise.

Maya Angelou

Characters

In order of appearance

ACT ONE
(1862)
SARAH BONETTA, *African, nineteen years old*
AGGIE, *a servant, African, forties*
JAMES DAVIES, *Sarah's husband, African, thirty-five years old*
MRS SCHOEN, *Sarah's guardian, fifties, white*
REVEREND VENN, *an unexpected guest, white, fifties*
HARRIET WALLER, *an unexpected guest, white, fifties*

ACT TWO
(Present day)
SARAH, *African origin, late thirties*
JAMES, *Sarah's husband, African origin, forty years old*
HARRIET, *an unexpected guest, white, forty years old*
BEN, *Harriet's husband, white, forty years old*

ACT THREE
(1897)
QUEEN VICTORIA, *white, forties*
SARAH BONETTA, *African, twenty-four years old*
SARAH, *African, late thirties*

Note on Text

A forward slash (/) indicates overlapping dialogue.

Dialogue in [square brackets] is intention, not to be spoken.

This text went to press before the end of rehearsals and so may differ slightly from the play as performed.

ACT ONE

The Davies Household, Brighton, 1862

A small, detached Georgian house with gardens.

Inside is crammed with expensive paintings and expensive ornaments sitting in expensive dressers. There are two large armchairs and a two-seater couch. In front of the two-seater couch is a small table. It has a white tablecloth with lace trim.

On the table sits an empty curate stand, a fine bone-china tea set, a teapot, a tea caddy, a cream jug, sugar bowl, a slop bowl, a tea strainer and side plates.

SARAH BONETTA, a fragile-looking teenager, sits on the two-seater couch. She wears a conservative black dress. AGGIE, a scruffy-looking maid sits beside her. They are both of African origin, dark in complexion.

AGGIE nervously mimes rinsing the empty teapot with boiling water and pours it into the slop bowl. She then mimes pouring some water into the newly rinsed teapot. Next she mimes putting a teaspoon full of tea into a cup and adding water. She allows this to steep for a minute or two and then adds more water. This, too, is a mime.

AGGIE (*attempts a posh accent*). How do you have your tea, ma'am?

A beat.

How do you have your tea, Mrs Davies?

SARAH BONETTA. I have it strong, with lemon and two lumps of sugar. Thank you.

AGGIE mimes adding more tea and mouths counting up to ten as the brew steeps longer. SARAH BONETTA catches her counting. AGGIE stops and instead counts in her head, nodding the numbers. She mimes adding the sugar and lemon and then hands the cup and saucer to SARAH.

Thank you, Agatha.

AGGIE *stifles her giggles*.

AGGIE. Sorry, ma'am, but no one calls me Agatha 'cept me mum and she's long since passed over. I mean, if she could see me now, sitting here, she'd have a fit. If she could, I mean.

SARAH BONETTA. Remember, Agatha, a good hostess is not distracted by anything.

AGGIE. Yes, ma'am. Sorry, ma'am. Mrs Davies, I mean.

SARAH BONETTA. Not even if there is a pistol shot or hurricane outside the front door.

AGGIE *giggles*.

AGGIE. A hurricane in Brighton. As if.

SARAH BONETTA *waits patiently for* AGGIE *to regain her composure*.

Would you like a scone, Mrs Davies? Or bread and butter?

SARAH BONETTA. I'll have some bread and butter. Thank you.

AGGIE *passes* SARAH BONETTA *the empty curate stand.* SARAH BONETTA *takes a plate, and mimes taking a piece of bread and butter from the curate stand and placing it on the plate.* AGGIE *mimes pouring herself a cup of tea. She counts to ten with nods and then adds a lump of imaginary sugar, and imaginary cream.*

They both mime drinking tea.

There is a very long silence.

As the hostess you must be the heartbeat of the conversation.

AGGIE. Yes, Mrs Davies.

SARAH BONETTA. You mustn't ever let it go flat.

AGGIE. No, Mrs Davies.

SARAH BONETTA. Because it's your responsibility entirely as to whether it will be a failure or a success and there will be talk of the unkind variety if the former. If there is a guest who begins to lead – which is clearly an indication of ill-breeding, and you should think hard about inviting that guest to tea again, unless they're important and you don't have a choice in the matter – you should allow him or her to have their way but you must regain your position as hostess at the very next opportunity.

AGGIE. Yes, ma'am. Sorry, ma'am. Yes, Mrs Davies.

A very long silence.

SARAH BONETTA. The key to a successful tea party is to talk about what you know.

AGGIE. Yes, Mrs Davies.

A long silence as AGGIE *tries to think of something. She opens her mouth and closes it again.*

Another silence.

The scones are delicious, ain't they?

SARAH BONETTA. Yes they are.

AGGIE. It's all in the butter.

SARAH BONETTA. Really?

AGGIE. Yes. I get the butter from the market on a Wednesday. Only cost ma'am a bob for two pound cos on a Wednesday One-eyed Ned likes to do a clear-out before it turns.

A pause.

SARAH BONETTA. Or you can remark on what one of your guests is wearing.

AGGIE. Yes, ma'am.

SARAH BONETTA. And remember to smile gently. Benevolently.

AGGIE manages a smile. It's more of a grimace.

Very good.

AGGIE takes an imaginary scone from the curate stand and goes to take an imaginary bite. SARAH BONETTA *stiffens.* AGGIE *stops and puts the scone on a side plate. She picks up the side plate with one hand and then picks up the imaginary scone with the other and then goes to take an imaginary bite.* SARAH BONETTA *freezes again.* AGGIE *stops, breaks the imaginary scone and then pops an*

imaginary piece of scone into her mouth. SARAH
BONETTA *relaxes, gives a little smile.* AGGIE *finishes
chewing the imaginary piece of scone. This is followed by
another long silence.*

JAMES DAVIES *enters from upstairs and observes them
with mild amusement.* JAMES *is African with strong African
features. He is so striking and so immaculately groomed that
he practically shines. He carries a pipe.*

AGGIE. I like your dress it's –

AGGIE *notices* JAMES *and is visibly affected by his
presence.*

SARAH BONETTA. Carry on.

AGGIE. I like your dress, Mrs Davies.

SARAH BONETTA. Thank you.

They drink in silence. AGGIE*'s cup and saucer clatter wildly.*

Remember, when all else fails or when things become
awkward…

AGGIE *draws a blank. Then she remembers.*

AGGIE. Yes, Mrs Davies. Righto.

A pause.

It's a nice afternoon, ain't it?

SARAH BONETTA. Yes, it's quite pleasant. It makes a welcome
change from last week. Last week was a constant drizzle.

AGGIE. Yes.

A pause.

SARAH BONETTA. Of course, a constant drizzle is quite
irritating. One never quite knows what to wear because it
might ease up or it might not and then one gets stuck.

AGGIE. Yes. One never does.

A pause.

I'm very fond of drizzle.

SARAH BONETTA. Really? Why's that?

AGGIE. Well, cos of why you said you was.

SARAH BONETTA. But I'm not.

AGGIE. Not what, ma'am?

SARAH BONETTA. Fond of drizzle.

AGGIE. Who is, ma'am?

SARAH BONETTA. Very good, Aggie. That's enough for now. Why don't you see to the cakes?

AGGIE. Yes, ma'am.

AGGIE quickly gets up, relieved, curtsies, but, in her haste, knocks the curate stand from the table.

Shit. Sorry, ma'am. Mrs Davies. Shit. Ma'am.

AGGIE puts the curate stand back on the table, looking nervously at JAMES as she exits into the kitchen. JAMES applauds as he lights his pipe.

JAMES. Bravo. She's utterly abysmal.

SARAH BONETTA. She isn't supposed to be abysmal.

JAMES. Oh really?

SARAH BONETTA. She has to perform perfectly.

JAMES. I see. Perhaps it might have been easier all round if you'd started with something simple like a spot of English or mathematics. With mathematics one knows where one stands.

SARAH BONETTA. The nuns will teach them all of that. Etiquette is something only I know. Besides, the Queen will adore it.

JAMES. You do realise that out there we will be laws unto ourselves?

SARAH BONETTA. Yes but I still prefer to have the Queen's blessing.

A pause.

If we had a few more days Aggie would be perfect.

The sound of something smashing comes from the kitchen.

JAMES. Just a few?

AGGIE *pokes her head through the door.*

AGGIE. It's all right, ma'am. No need for a panic. That weren't your best china.

SARAH BONETTA. Thank you, Aggie.

AGGIE *disappears back into the kitchen.* SARAH *goes to the window and looks out.*

She's late.

JAMES. The three o'clock is hardly ever on time. It's a shame the other maid isn't here.

SARAH BONETTA. She would have been if you hadn't made her nervous.

JAMES. How did I make her nervous? I hardly spoke to her.

SARAH BONETTA. When you did she found it disconcerting. She was enamoured, my dear. They both are.

JAMES. Don't be ridiculous.

SARAH BONETTA. A woman knows these things.

JAMES. She does, does she?

JAMES *takes* SARAH*'s hand.*

I can't tell you how comforted I am that you've taken to the idea of settling in Africa so readily.

SARAH BONETTA *quickly withdraws from him.*

SARAH BONETTA. Mama will be here soon and I have yet to turn down her bed.

JAMES. Leave that to the girl.

SARAH BONETTA. She really can't be expected to do everything.

The doorbell sounds. Another clatter from the kitchen.

JAMES. If she could do just one thing I would be eternally grateful.

SARAH BONETTA *can barely contain her excitement as she nervously plumps up cushions and rearranges ornaments. She runs to a hanging mirror and checks her face.*

SARAH BONETTA. I still can't decide whether she should have a view of the sea or the garden.

JAMES. Whatever one you choose, she'll criticise.

SARAH BONETTA. Mama doesn't –

AGGIE comes out, flustered, and heads for the hallway.

Aggie, slowly.

AGGIE. Yes, ma'am.

SARAH BONETTA. And tuck in your blouse.

AGGIE. Yes, ma'am.

AGGIE tucks in her blouse and exits down the hallway with exaggerated slowness.

As SARAH BONETTA turns away she stumbles over a propped-up painting. She picks it up, examines it.

SARAH BONETTA. Perhaps this *should* come with us. Oh, I really don't know.

AGGIE enters with MRS SCHOEN, a slim, matronly type woman with a severe face – although beneath the brusqueness is kindness. SARAH BONETTA runs up to her and embraces her.

Mama!

MRS SCHOEN allows herself the luxury of an affectionate hug before quickly extracting herself.

MRS SCHOEN. Careful, you'll have us tumbling to the ground.

SARAH BONETTA. I have missed you terribly!

MRS SCHOEN. Don't be silly, my dear.

SARAH BONETTA. I've been in a state of mental misery. Haven't I, James?

JAMES. She really has.

SARAH BONETTA. It's been absolute torture.

JAMES. Well, I hope not entirely.

MRS SCHOEN. She's clearly not busy enough for such mawkishness.

SARAH BONETTA. I have been busy, / Mama.

MRS SCHOEN. How are you, James?

SARAH BONETTA. But it's very / different here.

JAMES. Very well. Thank you.

SARAH BONETTA. David and Lottie don't write as often as they promised and I hardly hear from Princess Alice.

MRS SCHOEN. That's what usually happens when one marries.

MRS SCHOEN *gives her an appraising look.*

Etta, you know black doesn't become you.

SARAH BONETTA. I'm abandoning colours for the Queen.

MRS SCHOEN. That's all very well and good but you simply don't stand out.

MRS SCHOEN *goes to smooth down* SARAH BONETTA*'s hair and has difficulty with it.*

SARAH BONETTA. Mama, it's already / flattened.

MRS SCHOEN. The russet. Do you still have the russet with the black-velvet trim?

SARAH BONETTA. Mama – [stop]!

MRS SCHOEN. Etta, we have guests.

A pause.

SARAH BONETTA. What type of guests?

MRS SCHOEN. The usual sort.

SARAH BONETTA. Oh no, Mama!

MRS SCHOEN. It couldn't be helped.

SARAH BONETTA. But, Mama, I wanted to –

MRS SCHOEN. Please don't make a fuss, dear. They'll soon be here.

SARAH BONETTA *has a coughing fit.*

She needs water.

JAMES. Aggie, please fetch her a glass.

AGGIE *heads for the kitchen.*

SARAH BONETTA. I'm all right, Aggie. Will you take Mama's bag to her room?

AGGIE *heads in the opposite direction.*

It's the front one. The one with the sea view. Unless you would rather –

SARAH BONETTA *coughs again.*

MRS SCHOEN (*to* AGGIE). Fetch her some water, please!

AGGIE *stops in her tracks, unsure which orders to follow.* MRS SCHOEN *looks sternly at* AGGIE. AGGIE *runs out to the kitchen.*

Where's your tincture?

SARAH BONETTA. Mama –

MRS SCHOEN. James, where is it?

JAMES. I believe it got misplaced with the move down.

MRS SCHOEN. Well, why didn't you ask me to send you some more?

MRS SCHOEN *gets out a small bottle from her purse.*

(*To* SARAH BONETTA.) You are your own worst enemy.

SARAH BONETTA. It doesn't have any effect anyway.

MRS SCHOEN. Of course it has an effect. Father had a dreadful cold last week and it has improved considerably.

SARAH BONETTA. He has a cold every November. One which would improve all on its own if given the chance.

MRS SCHOEN. One teaspoonful three times a day.

SARAH BONETTA. James, have I told you how Dr Jenner used to order me to sleep with a handful of cloves on my chest? The result was an aversion to apple pie.

MRS SCHOEN. If he's good enough for the Queen. Open.

SARAH BONETTA *reluctantly opens her mouth and* MRS
SCHOEN *drops the tincture on her tongue.* SARAH
BONETTA *grimaces.*

This one has turmeric in it.

JAMES. I've heard good things about turmeric.

MRS SCHOEN *touches* SARAH BONETTA*'s forehead.*

MRS SCHOEN. Is she taking her walks?

SARAH BONETTA. She is. Every day. Seven o'clock
promptly before prayers.

MRS SCHOEN. Africa will be good for you.

SARAH BONETTA. So everyone says.

MRS SCHOEN. Be a good girl and put on the russet.

SARAH BONETTA *heads upstairs as* AGGIE *returns from
the kitchen.*

SARAH BONETTA (*to* AGGIE). I thought I told you to take
Mama's bag upstairs.

AGGIE. She ain't come with one, ma'am.

SARAH BONETTA. What do you mean she hasn't come
with one?

AGGIE. Well, I ain't seen it.

A beat.

MRS SCHOEN. Now don't fuss. You know when Father's
unwell –

SARAH BONETTA. You promised to stay for a few days.

MRS SCHOEN. Sarah, there are far more important matters to
be concerned with.

SARAH BONETTA. Yes, the russet dress. Of course.

SARAH BONETTA *exits.*

There is a long silence.

JAMES. How did you find the trip?

MRS SCHOEN. Comfortable.

JAMES. I do like a trip by train. I have had the most peculiar conversations.

MRS SCHOEN. I can imagine.

A pause.

I did try to shake them off in Gillingham but they were overwhelmingly persistent.

MRS SCHOEN *begins to tidy up for a bit.*

Was this really the best house you could find in the village?

JAMES. Of those who would let to us, yes.

MRS SCHOEN *continues to tidy up. It is fruitless.*

MRS SCHOEN. You did tell them who you were?

JAMES. They already knew. Moreover, they took pains to tell us how they'd all come down to the parade to catch a sight of the wedding. They congratulated us profusely.

MRS SCHOEN *digests this. She examines some of the paintings.*

She's really at a loss as to what to leave behind. She adores every gift.

MRS SCHOEN. Well, you'll just have to be brutal.

A pause.

JAMES. These guests –

MRS SCHOEN. All very irritating but there was no choice in the matter.

JAMES. Do you know them well?

MRS SCHOEN. Well, we know the Reverend, of course.

JAMES. The Reverend? I thought you said they were the usual sort?

MRS SCHOEN. At times I find it impossible to distinguish between the usual and the Reverend. Between you and I, I'm quite peeved with the Reverend for foisting a complete stranger upon us.

JAMES. If it's for the Society.

MRS SCHOEN. It always is.

JAMES. So did they want to see the sights?

MRS SCHOEN. Aggie? Is that your name?

AGGIE. Yes, ma'am.

MRS SCHOEN. Go up and assist Mrs Davies.

AGGIE. Yes, ma'am.

    AGGIE *bobs and exits*.

MRS SCHOEN. What a peculiar creature. Where did you find her?

JAMES. She's from Croydon, I believe.

MRS SCHOEN. Croydon?

JAMES. Well, we can only take her word for it.

MRS SCHOEN. She seems rather inexperienced.

JAMES. Well, she's more of a cook than maid.

MRS SCHOEN. So where's the maid?

JAMES. We don't have one at present.

MRS SCHOEN. I'm sorry?

JAMES. She left. Martha.

MRS SCHOEN. Why?

JAMES. She found living here rather difficult. I thought Sarah might have mentioned this?

MRS SCHOEN. No she did not mention this.

JAMES. Finding both a cook and a maid has been quite an exercise.

MRS SCHOEN. How many answered the advert? I presume you placed one in the local paper.

JAMES. Of course we did. Two replied.

MRS SCHOEN. Two?

JAMES. Martha was by far the best, believe me.

MRS SCHOEN. So now there's just Aggie?

JAMES. Yes.

A pause.

MRS SCHOEN. She strikes me as fidgety.

JAMES. I believe that's nothing more than nerves.

MRS SCHOEN. Over what?

JAMES. Us. Well, me if you must know. Sarah seems to believe that I'm the object of their affections.

MRS SCHOEN. Their affections?

JAMES. Yes.

MRS SCHOEN. You do know Sarah is quite inexperienced in these matters?

A pause.

No, I've seen the sort before. Have you references?

JAMES. Not yet. We sent for them as soon as we moved in.

MRS SCHOEN. It's been three weeks. Three weeks is more than enough time for an answer.

Be sure Sarah is keeping an inventory of what's in this household.

JAMES. She really is quite / harmless.

MRS SCHOEN. I really should have taken more of an interest.

The doorbell goes.

We shall make this quick and painless. Does the girl know what to do?

JAMES. Yes.

MRS SCHOEN. At least that's something.

A pause.

JAMES. They can't have seen much, can they?

MRS SCHOEN. Seen much of what?

JAMES. The sights.

MRS SCHOEN. What sights?

JAMES. You said they went sightseeing.

MRS SCHOEN. No, I didn't.

JAMES. Oh, so why are they behind?

MRS SCHOEN. Because they walked.

JAMES. They walked?

MRS SCHOEN. Yes.

JAMES. They walked all the way from the station?

MRS SCHOEN. That's correct.

JAMES. But it's two miles.

A beat.

Uphill.

MRS SCHOEN. Well you know how much I like walking and the Reverend was perfectly fine.

JAMES. And his companion?

In the hallway a conversation can be heard.

REVEREND VENN (*off*). Will you fetch Mrs Waller a glass of water?

MRS WALLER (*off*). No, no. I'm quite all – all –

REVEREND VENN (*off*). Quick, girl. Quick.

MRS SCHOEN. How else could I give you sufficient notice?

AGGIE hurries through the parlour towards the kitchen.

I thought she knew what to do?

JAMES. Aggie, will you please announce the guests?

AGGIE. Sorry, Mr Davies. It's Mr –

A beat.

AGGIE heads back out to the hallway just as REVEREND VENN and MRS WALLER enter. MRS WALLER is a rotund-looking lady and is panting for breath.

REVEREND VENN. Do you have the water, girl?

AGGIE. Yes, sir. I mean, no, sir. (*To* JAMES *and* MRS SCHOEN.) It's your guests.

AGGIE bobs and heads for the kitchen.

MRS WALLER. I'm really quite –

REVEREND VENN. Breathe out, my dear. Breathe out.

JAMES. How are you, Reverend?

REVEREND VENN. Good, good, old boy. Splendid.

JAMES. What's this I hear about you walking two miles?

MRS SCHOEN. Two miles, was it? I didn't think it was two miles. James, your directions weren't very clear.

JAMES. My directions?

MRS SCHOEN. I am so sorry. I most certainly would've suggested we hail a cab if I thought it was going to be two miles. Please accept my deepest apologies.

REVEREND VENN. Oh, don't apologise to me, Mrs Schoen. I'm quite amenable to a good walk. It's Mrs Waller I was more concerned about.

MRS WALLER. I'm quite –

REVEREND VENN. Deep breaths, Mrs Waller. Deep breaths. She wasn't used to it and it all being uphill. Straight ahead! Straight ahead!

MRS SCHOEN. I really thought it was!

REVEREND VENN. Shot off like a racehorse.

MRS SCHOEN. I kept thinking. Any minute now and I'd see the house up ahead but I never did.

REVEREND VENN. James, old boy, your directions are quite dire.

JAMES. I believe I might have mentioned something about living at the top of a hill.

MRS WALLER. Honestly, it's quite –

REVEREND VENN. Deep breaths, Mrs Waller. What on earth is the girl doing out there?

JAMES. Perhaps you might have allowed Mrs Waller the bench under the old birch? The walk's not as strenuous with the odd reprieve.

REVEREND VENN. I did. But I was mindful of losing the way especially when I could see Mrs Schoen's figure vanishing rapidly into the distance.

MRS SCHOEN. I really thought you were keeping up.

AGGIE enters with the glass of water. Hands it to MRS WALLER. *AGGIE exits.*

MRS WALLER. Thank you.

MRS WALLER takes a gulp. She begins to catch her breath.

JAMES. At least you didn't get lost.

REVEREND VENN. Can you imagine if we had?

MRS SCHOEN. Yes.

REVEREND VENN. Still, nothing lost. Where's the Princess?

MRS SCHOEN. The Princess will be down when she's ready.

There is an awkward silence as they notice MRS WALLER *observing* JAMES.

REVEREND VENN. Mrs Waller, I'd like you to meet Mr James Davies.

JAMES steps forward, holds out his hand. MRS WALLER *takes his hand carefully, a mixture of curiosity and excitement.*

JAMES. How do you do, Mrs Waller?

MRS WALLER. Delighted.

JAMES. I shan't enquire after your journey.

They all laugh.

However, I do apologise for the muddle as it appears to be entirely my fault.

MRS WALLER. It's quite all right. I rather enjoyed the views. They're quite spectacular.

JAMES. They are, aren't they?

MRS WALLER. If it wasn't for the hill, I believe I would've kept up.

REVEREND VENN. I believe you really would, Mrs Waller.

A silence.

AGGIE *enters, clears her throat.*

AGGIE. Ladies and gentlemen, please be uprising and upstanding for her royalty Princess Sarah Forbes Bonetta Davies.

SARAH, *dressed in the russet and jewels, enters.* MRS WALLER *gasps, impressed.* REVEREND VENN *takes* SARAH*'s hand and kisses it lavishly.*

REVEREND VENN. How are you, my dear?

SARAH BONETTA. Quite well.

REVEREND VENN. Good, good. Splendid. The sea air certainly agrees with you.

SARAH BONETTA. Thank you.

REVEREND VENN. I apologise for such an impromptu visit. I hope we aren't going to be too much of a nuisance?

SARAH BONETTA. Not at all, Reverend. I was just saying to my husband how much I miss having guests and then three arrive all at once.

REVEREND VENN. Good, good. Mrs Davies, I'd like you to meet the esteemed Mrs Harriet Waller.

SARAH BONETTA *holds out her hand.*

MRS WALLER *gets up and does a very low curtsy and stays low for a very, very long time. Everyone exchanges uncomfortable glances.*

SARAH BONETTA. You may rise.

MRS WALLER *attempts to rise but clearly needs help.* JAMES *and* REVEREND VENN *go to her aid. She instinctively recoils from* JAMES *and accepts the help of* REVEREND VENN.

MRS WALLER. I do apologise. I must still be –

REVEREND VENN. Fatigued.

MRS WALLER. Yes.

> MRS WALLER *is seated. Gets her breath. She stares in awe at* SARAH BONETTA.

SARAH BONETTA. We were about to have tea. Would you both like to join us?

MRS WALLER. Well, if I'm not intruding.

SARAH BONETTA. You wouldn't be.

JAMES. Not at all.

MRS SCHOEN. Not when you've come all this way after all.

REVEREND VENN. Good, good. Splendid. Shall we sit?

SARAH BONETTA. Yes. Let's.

> SARAH *proceeds to sit down. They all follow* SARAH*'s lead but there aren't enough chairs.*

REVEREND VENN. I shall stand.

JAMES. Don't be silly. I'll stand.

MRS SCHOEN. You really should sit down, Reverend.

REVEREND VENN. I shall stand. I'm used to standing. I've given sermons that have gone on for hours.

MRS SCHOEN. Yes. You have.

JAMES. Sit down, Reverend. We'll bring in another chair.

MRS WALLER. I really have put you all at an inconvenience.

JAMES. Nonsense.

SARAH BONETTA. Of course you haven't.

MRS SCHOEN. Not at all.

SARAH BONETTA. Aggie, will you bring down another chair?

AGGIE. Yes, ma'am.

REVEREND VENN. Good, good.

> *A beat.*

AGGIE. Which one, ma'am?

JAMES. Fetch one from the drawing room.

AGGIE. Yes, Mr Davies.

SARAH BONETTA. Those chairs are far too heavy for one person, dear.

JAMES. Yes, they're certainly a two-man job.

MRS SCHOEN. Well, if we had two men to hand perhaps it could be done.

JAMES. I believe it could.

A beat.

Yes, yes, of course. Reverend?

REVEREND VENN. Oh yes. Yes. Good.

JAMES *and* REVEREND VENN *get up and exit.*

SARAH BONETTA (*to* AGGIE). You can bring in the tea.

AGGIE (*nervous*). The tea, ma'am?

SARAH BONETTA. Yes.

AGGIE *bobs and exits. A short silence.*

How was the trip down, Mrs Waller?

MRS WALLER. Oh very good.

SARAH BONETTA. And did you enjoy your walk up to the house?

MRS WALLER. It was a splendid walk, Princess Bonetta.

SARAH BONETTA. On a good day you can see quite a distance.

MRS WALLER. Yes. I did remark on the vista to the Reverend.

A pause.

SARAH BONETTA. You must tell us exactly how this visit came about, Mrs Waller. Mama has yet to explain.

MRS WALLER. It was quite a coincidence, actually. It's an interesting story. I – Perhaps I should wait for the Reverend to explain.

SARAH BONETTA. It sounds rather intriguing.

MRS SCHOEN. I don't think they'll be too / [long].

MRS WALLER. All I'll say is I happened quite coincidentally to be visiting St Olave's Church Orphanage when we bumped into each other.

SARAH BONETTA. Oh, so you know the Reverend well?

MRS WALLER. I was a member of his parish before he gave it up.

SARAH BONETTA. Mama, I'm surprised that you and Mrs Waller haven't met before, given that you're also involved with the orphanage.

MRS SCHOEN. Mrs Waller tells me she's only recently become involved.

MRS WALLER. Not that I hadn't wanted to become involved much earlier but the Lancashire unemployed have been quite demanding. But we must do all we can.

SARAH BONETTA. Yes, we must.

MRS SCHOEN. And now Africa.

MRS WALLER. Yes.

MRS SCHOEN. On top of the unemployed and the orphanage.

MRS WALLER. Well, I'm hoping Africa won't be too strenuous.

SARAH BONETTA. You were saying you were at the orphanage.

MRS WALLER. Yes, I was at the orphanage and the Reverend mentioned in passing that he planned to pay Mrs Schoen a visit so I asked, you know, by way of conversation, whether he was speaking of the Mrs Schoen that was the guardian of Sarah Forbes Bonetta, to whom my family is connected.

A beat.

I don't mean a blood connection, of course. I really should wait for the Reverend.

SARAH BONETTA. Well now I'm really / intrigued.

MRS WALLER. You see, my late husband and I are very good friends with the Millses of Ockshott who are dear friends of the Greens of Chesham who are cousins of the Laneys in Preston. The Laneys have a cousin in Bath, a Donald Smith-Butts who is the second cousin twice removed of Lady Mary Pearce of Stanmore who knows the Phipps quite well.

A pause.

MRS SCHOEN. The Phipps of?

SARAH BONETTA. The Phipps.

A beat.

Our Phipps, Mama. The Phipps of St James.

MRS SCHOEN. Oh our Phipps! Of course! So you know the Phipps?

MRS WALLER. In a roundabout way, yes.

JAMES *and* REVEREND VENN *enter with the chair.*

REVEREND VENN. Left. Left. Careful. Left. Stop! Splendid.

MRS WALLER. What a magnificent chair!

SARAH BONETTA. Thank you.

The men put down the chair and sit down.

MRS WALLER. Everything in this room is a veritable feast for the eyes.

SARAH BONETTA. Thank you. Unfortunately, we're packing so the house isn't quite as one would want.

MRS WALLER. I remember when my late husband and I were newlyweds. We were always busy.

A beat.

REVEREND VENN. Has Mrs Waller mentioned all the charitable work she undertakes?

MRS WALLER. Reverend, please –

REVEREND VENN. I simply must extol your virtues. Not only is Mrs Waller a philanthropist but she is also quite the visionary.

MRS WALLER. Well, I'm afraid this visionary has let the cat out of the bag.

REVEREND VENN. Cat out of what bag, Mrs Waller?

MRS WALLER. My connection with the Princess.

REVEREND VENN. Oh yes.

JAMES. You're connected?

MRS SCHOEN. Not by blood.

MRS WALLER. No.

JAMES. That would be difficult to explain.

They laugh.

MRS SCHOEN. I just hope I can remember the chain of connection.

MRS WALLER. Oh, it's quite easy, Mrs Schoen. My late husband and I are very good friends with the Millses of Ockshott –

MRS SCHOEN. Yes. And the Mills are related to the Greens.

MRS WALLER. No, not related to. Just dear friends of.

MRS SCHOEN. Terribly sorry.

JAMES. And the Greens are?

MRS WALLER. Cousins of the Laneys in Preston. The Laneys have a cousin in Bath – a Donald Smith-Butts – and Donald Smith-Butts is the second cousin twice removed of Lady Mary Pearce of Stanmore.

REVEREND VENN. It's Lady Mary Pearce who knows the Phipps. Mrs Schoen, I believe you've met Lady Mary Pearce?

MRS SCHOEN. No, I don't think I have.

REVEREND VENN. Really?

A beat.

Well, it's quite fortuitous that you and Mrs Waller have met then!

SARAH BONETTA. To think, Mama, if you had left for the train just a few moments earlier you would have missed our guests entirely.

MRS SCHOEN. Yes. To think!

A pause.

JAMES. I wonder if one might simply mention Mrs Waller's connection to Lady Mary Pearce instead of going through the entire list. It would be disastrous if one got the sequence wrong.

MRS WALLER. Perhaps we should write it down.

REVEREND VENN. Champion idea. Who has a pen?

No one does. SARAH *rings the bell. They all wait for a moment.* AGGIE *brings in the hot water and extra cups and saucers. The cups and saucers rattle as she sets them out.*

AGGIE. Tea, ma'am.

SARAH BONETTA. Will you get us a pen and paper?

AGGIE. Now, ma'am?

SARAH BONETTA. Yes.

AGGIE (*relieved*).Yes, ma'am. Thank you, ma'am.

AGGIE *bobs and exits.*

SARAH BONETTA. What business is it you're in, Mrs Waller?

MRS WALLER. Soap. Medicated.

MRS SCHOEN. How wonderful.

JAMES. We all need soap.

REVEREND VENN. That we do.

MRS WALLER. Waller Carbolic. Perhaps you might have heard of us?

REVEREND VENN. Of course we have.

SARAH BONETTA/JAMES. Yes.

MRS WALLER. We've been established since 1820. We consider our main competitors to be Pears.

MRS SCHOEN. Pears. Yes. I've heard of Pears.

JAMES. Pears is an excellent soap.

REVEREND VENN. As is Waller Carbolic.

JAMES. Yes.

MRS WALLER. We also produce a luxury bar. If I'd known I'd be sitting here with Princess Sarah Forbes Bonetta and her husband I would have brought you all a hamper. I'll send each of you one as soon as I'm home.

SARAH BONETTA. That's very kind of you.

JAMES. Thank you.

MRS SCHOEN. Thank you, very much.

REVEREND VENN. Good. Splendid.

SARAH BONETTA. How do you take your tea, Mrs Waller?

MRS WALLER. Not too sweet. Four sugars.

SARAH BONETTA *serves* MRS WALLER *and the others their tea.*

SARAH BONETTA. You must tell us what brought about your interest in the Society, Mrs Waller.

MRS WALLER. Well, Your Majesty –

SARAH BONETTA. Sarah, please.

MRS WALLER. Well, Sarah, I believe the natives ought to learn how to look after themselves. That way they'll be able to come up. The Reverend tells me that your husband plans to employ the natives. Teach them commerce. I believe that they are quite capable of it.

REVEREND VENN. Give a man a fish and he will eat for a day.

MRS WALLER. Teach a man to fish…

REVEREND VENN. That's why it was imperative she meet you, James, before you left.

MRS WALLER. Yes. The Reverend says you made your fortune as a sea merchant.

JAMES. I served as a lieutenant on *HMS Volcano*. After the navy I began trading along the Gold Coast.

MRS WALLER. Well I am impressed.

REVEREND VENN. James, go on.

JAMES. Mrs Waller, I've recently purchased a palm-oil farm where, indeed, I do intend to take on young apprentices.

They will learn accountancy and management so that each of them will have the same level of expertise as I. They in turn shall leave the farm and set up their own businesses and will, in turn, teach other young men their skills. In this way they will be able to manage the natural resources themselves once the British leave the protectorate. Of course, I am unable to undertake this venture entirely with my own capital so I'm asking for the interest of a few highly regarded investors.

MRS WALLER. My son says the French are putting palm oil in everything so we'd better get in or we'll sink.

REVEREND VENN. He's spot on, Mrs Waller. Spot on.

JAMES. It's a solid investment. The market for palm oil is quite buoyant.

MRS WALLER. Can I just say, you both look quite different to your photographs.

A beat.

REVEREND VENN. Photographs never do one justice, do they?

MRS WALLER. No.

SARAH BONETTA. We always come across as quite serious and quite flat. I hope we're more animated in person, Mrs Waller?

MRS WALLER. Yes. Yes, you are.

REVEREND VENN. I had one taken recently with my two granddaughters. They distort one quite considerably I think. It's all to do with the correct lighting. You have to find someone rather experienced, old boy. Have any old Tom or Dick do it and you're left in a bit of a stink.

JAMES. Well someone better inform *Britannia* and *The Illustrated*.

They laugh.

AGGIE *enters with the curate stand, which is now full of cakes and sandwiches.*

Ah, here she is with the pen.

A beat.

AGGIE. Yes, Mr Davies.

She puts the curate stand down and exits.

A beat.

JAMES. No matter. I must have one somewhere.

JAMES gets up and looks. In their own time, they take a sandwich or a scone and place the food on their plates.

MRS WALLER. So when will you be off to Africa?

JAMES. In two weeks.

MRS WALLER. How thrilling!

SARAH BONETTA. Will you want to visit Lagos at all, Mrs Waller?

MRS WALLER. Good heavens, no! But I admire greatly the missionaries who venture out there. The sacrifices they make…

MRS SCHOEN. I'd have thought you might have wanted to go given your planned investment.

MRS WALLER. Of course. Perhaps if I didn't have so many responsibilities here…

REVEREND VENN. And it is difficult to give up one's creature comforts for pursuits of the unknown.

MRS WALLER. Well, I'm not one for the heat.

REVEREND VENN. Neither am I, Mrs Waller. Neither am I.

MRS SCHOEN. Yet you go to Africa twice a year.

REVEREND VENN. One eventually gets used to it.

JAMES. Sarah and I are currently involved in beastly negotiations as to what gifts to take and what to leave behind.

MRS SCHOEN. But choose she must.

MRS WALLER. You're quite fortunate to have such wonderful possessions. You must cherish your wife, considerably.

JAMES. I'm afraid I can't take all the credit, Mrs Waller. They're gifts from Her Majesty.

A beat.

REVEREND VENN. I suggest you categorise them in order of importance.

SARAH BONETTA. They're all equally important.

REVEREND VENN. Gifts that are useful versus gifts that are ornamental.

JAMES. A champion idea!

SARAH BONETTA. Whether frivolous or practical they are all of sentimental value.

MRS WALLER. I'm surprised you're so calm about going back, Sarah. Given your history.

SARAH BONETTA. As the Reverend says, one gets used to things.

MRS WALLER. I have to say, I caught one of the first readings of *Dahomey and the Dahomans* ten years ago…

REVEREND VENN. A phenomenal / book.

MRS WALLER. And I've been avidly keeping abreast of your story.

SARAH BONETTA. Thank you.

MRS WALLER. When Commander Forbes read the passage of how he rescued you from those savages I could practically hear those beating drums myself. It was just so evocative. I always wanted to know, as Commander Forbes never said, but were you under some form of intoxication? I always wondered why any one of you didn't climb out of those baskets?

SARAH BONETTA. I don't really remember.

MRS WALLER. Well, I just want to say, you must have been the bravest little native in the world's entire existence.

SARAH BONETTA. Thank you.

MRS WALLER. I would've just been absolutely terrified.

A pause.

MRS SCHOEN. These scones are quite / [delicious] –

MRS WALLER. To know that at any moment you were about to be devoured alive.

SARAH BONETTA. Well, not [alive] –

MRS WALLER. Your royal African blood drunk by those frightful savages. Your tiny limbs torn apart and scattered amongst them to feast on like pigs on fodder.

REVEREND VENN. Did I mention Mrs Waller is quite the fanatic?

MRS SCHOEN. No, I don't think you did.

MRS WALLER. Well, it's such a fantastical tale! One minute you're about to be eaten alive and the next you're being rescued by –

SARAH BONETTA. I wasn't about to be eaten.

MRS WALLER. Oh.

A beat.

Are you quite sure?

SARAH BONETTA. Yes.

REVEREND VENN. I don't think Commander Forbes wrote 'eaten', did he? Did he write 'eaten'?

MRS SCHOEN. I don't think he did write 'eaten'.

MRS WALLER. But there are some of them that do go for cannibalism?

REVEREND VENN. Yes. Some believe it prevents smallpox. Others do it to seek an ancestral blessing.

MRS WALLER. Well I haven't got it completely wrong then.

SARAH BONETTA. But *I* wasn't about to be eaten, Mrs Waller.

MRS WALLER. You're quite sure? After all you were quite young.

SARAH BONETTA. I remember that.

MRS WALLER. Oh, well you must be right then.

A pause.

REVEREND VENN. Eaten. Not eaten. The method of how one is sacrificed is often superfluous.

JAMES. I'd rather be shot than boiled alive.

MRS WALLER. Were they boiled then?

MRS SCHOEN/JAMES. No!

Silence.

AGGIE *enters with the pen and paper.*

JAMES. Ah, the pen!

MRS SCHOEN. The pen!

REVEREND VENN. The pen!

AGGIE *hands the pen and jotting paper to* JAMES *and exits.* JAMES *hesitates.*

JAMES. What did we want the pen for?

MRS SCHOEN. Mrs Waller's connection.

JAMES. Ah yes.

A pause.

MRS WALLER. Would you like me to recap?

MRS SCHOEN. No.

JAMES. I believe I have it.

JAMES *begins to write. There is a long silence.*

MRS SCHOEN. Reverend, have you managed to read the news today?

REVEREND VENN. Yes. Yes. It's jolly good.

MRS WALLER. I'm afraid I – ?

REVEREND VENN. America.

JAMES. The win at Sharpsburg.

MRS WALLER. Oh yes.

> MRS WALLER *still looks blank*.

JAMES. The Unionists won.

MRS WALLER. Yes.

REVEREND VENN. The beginning of the end.

MRS SCHOEN. You're being far too optimistic. An end to the war does not necessarily mean an end to slavery.

REVEREND VENN. Of course it does.

MRS SCHOEN. We've outlawed slavery and a hundred years later America still hasn't followed suit.

JAMES. That's only because the Americans can't stand the thought of the English doing anything first.

MRS SCHOEN. Even if they're defeated, I think the Confederates will find a way of pursuing what they want.

REVEREND VENN. Not if it's against the law.

MRS SCHOEN. Yes and no one has ever flouted the law. Lest we forget the West Indies.

REVEREND VENN. The West Indies!

JAMES. Why did you have to mention the West Indies, Mrs Schoen?

REVEREND VENN. The most licentious, libellous, disagreeable race ever to grace the Earth. The plantation owners treat their workers like slaves.

MRS SCHOEN. My point exactly.

JAMES (*to* MRS WALLER). The West Indian plantation owners always set the Reverend off.

REVEREND VENN. Those people are beyond saving. They're worse than the Americans.

MRS SCHOEN. Yes. Etta, will you refresh the tea. Etta?

> SARAH *gathers herself and checks the tea*.

REVEREND VENN. To subjugate one man beneath another by virtue of race is morally reprehensible.

A sudden rap at the window startles everyone.

What on earth – ?

REVEREND VENN *goes to look out of the window.*

JAMES (*re: the window*). It's just the locals. They like to remind us of their presence once in a while.

SARAH BONETTA. Would anyone like another scone?

MRS SCHOEN. Yes, I would. Thank you.

SARAH BONETTA. Reverend, come away from the window or you'll make matters worse.

MRS WALLER. Why? What will they do?

SARAH BONETTA. Reverend?

MRS SCHOEN *helps herself to a scone. During the bedlam,* MRS WALLER *takes a teaspoon and conceals it about her person.*

REVEREND VENN. I can see one of them. He's got a thick red thatch of hair.

MRS SCHOEN. Come away from the window, Reverend.

MRS WALLER. Do you know who these people are?

SARAH BONETTA. There are at least five of them. They seem to enjoy congregating by the water trough. Would you like a scone, Reverend?

MRS WALLER. Why would they rattle the window?

REVEREND VENN. I'm going to have a word.

JAMES. I already have, Reverend. Several times.

REVEREND VENN. A man of the cloth, old boy.

REVEREND VENN *heads for the exit.*

Hold the fort! I shall be back in time to have another slice of Madeira cake.

MRS SCHOEN. James, do go with him.

JAMES follows REVEREND VENN *out. There is a short silence.*

I'm so pleased you've taken an interest in Africa, Mrs Waller.

MRS WALLER. I'm confident Mr Davies will do an excellent job. He's a Winchester boy after all.

SARAH BONETTA. He was educated in Sierra Leone by the Society.

MRS WALLER. Oh! I thought the papers said Winchester. He speaks incredibly well.

MRS SCHOEN. Mr Davies is a prime example of what the Church Missionary Society can achieve.

A pause.

SARAH BONETTA. Mama, what train do you intend to catch?

MRS SCHOEN. The twenty-past six.

MRS WALLER. I'll catch the twenty-past with you, Mrs Schoen, if I may.

MRS SCHOEN. That would be delightful.

SARAH BONETTA *rings the bell.*

MRS WALLER. Are you quite sure the Reverend will be safe?

SARAH BONETTA. Quite sure.

AGGIE *enters.*

Will you bring in some more hot water?

AGGIE. Yes, ma'am.

SARAH BONETTA. And perhaps you might fill the curate stand.

AGGIE. Yes, ma'am.

AGGIE *picks up the teapot and curate stand, they clatter against each other.*

SARAH BONETTA. It's all right. There won't be a performance today.

AGGIE. Yes, ma'am. Thank you, ma'am.

AGGIE *exits*.

SARAH BONETTA. I've heard all about the benefits of palm oil, Mrs Waller. How far do you see its versatility?

MRS WALLER. Forgive me if I'm being forward but I couldn't help overhearing you mentioning a performance? Please don't put anything off on my account. I've read so much about your talents.

SARAH BONETTA. I wasn't planning on giving a performance, Mrs Waller. It's just something I'd planned to show my mother.

MRS SCHOEN *is mildly surprised*.

I taught the maid how to take tea.

MRS WALLER. How marvellous! Why?

SARAH BONETTA. I'd like to perform more than my marital duties when I'm out there.

MRS WALLER. Well, of course, you're the Queen's protégée after all. You can't have all that intelligence go to waste.

SARAH BONETTA. I'd like to do my bit for the Society. Aggie is my first student.

MRS WALLER. Well that's very useful. African girls having afternoon tea. They drink that out there, do they?

SARAH BONETTA. Yes of course, Mrs Waller.

MRS WALLER. Etiquette... On top of them learning Scripture or how to sew and mend...

SARAH BONETTA. Yes. The Queen wants them to be as English as you or I, Mrs Waller.

MRS WALLER. Well, please don't put it off on my account. The performance.

MRS SCHOEN. It's fine. There's no need. The Queen has stated her wishes.

A pause.

MRS WALLER. I believe I read somewhere that you're quite the virtuoso at the pianoforte, Sarah. You played for Princess Alice a few years back.

SARAH BONETTA. Yes. That's right. For her birthday.

MRS WALLER. It would be wonderful to hear something.

A pause.

MRS SCHOEN. The piano's in the drawing room, isn't it?

SARAH BONETTA. Yes, it is.

MRS WALLER. I'd be quite happy to adjourn there.

SARAH BONETTA. I'd love to play something, Mrs Waller, really –

MRS WALLER. I wouldn't expect anything as grand as what you gave the Princess.

MRS SCHOEN. But the drawing room's filled with so many things, isn't it, Sarah? What with all the packing…

SARAH BONETTA. Yes, I'm afraid it is.

A pause.

MRS WALLER. I was just thinking about what you said, Mrs Schoen. About visiting the palm-oil farm before I invest. My son will visit, I'm sure. If I can persuade him, that is. You see, he's a very cautious investor. I didn't want to mention it before as I didn't want the men to think that I wasn't keen on the opportunity. I mean, if it were just down to me… But I assure you I'm completely behind it. The farm. Completely.

Silence.

MRS SCHOEN. The exercise with the maid, is it short?

SARAH BONETTA. Yes. Yes, it is.

MRS SCHOEN. Perhaps then we might see what you have done.

SARAH BONETTA. Yes, Mama.

AGGIE *enters with the hot water and the filled curate stand.* SARAH BONETTA *rinses the empty teapot with boiling water and pours it into the slop bowl. She then pours some water into the newly rinsed pot.*

Come and sit beside me, Aggie. I'd like you to serve us tea.

AGGIE *hesitates*.

It's just dear Mama and Mrs Waller.

AGGIE. Yes, ma'am.

AGGIE *takes a step towards* SARAH BONETTA *and faints*.

MRS WALLER. Is that part of it?

SARAH BONETTA *and* MRS SCHOEN *go to* AGGIE*'s aid and attempt to revive her.*

MRS SCHOEN (*to* SARAH BONETTA). Fetch the smelling salts.

SARAH BONETTA *exits*.

(*To* MRS WALLER.) Help me carry her to the chair.

MRS WALLER *is in shock*.

MRS SCHOEN. Mrs Waller?

MRS WALLER. Perhaps someone should fetch a doctor.

MRS SCHOEN. She doesn't need a doctor. She simply needs to be made comfortable.

MRS WALLER. I really think we should fetch a doctor.

MRS SCHOEN. There isn't one about.

A beat.

MRS WALLER. I'll see about the men.

MRS WALLER *exits into the hallway as* MRS SCHOEN *tries to revive* AGGIE. SARAH BONETTA *rushes back in, continues her search.*

MRS SCHOEN. Do you have the salts?

SARAH BONETTA. No. I'm sorry. I didn't think she was so nervous about it.

MRS SCHOEN. She will not do.

SARAH BONETTA. Where's Mrs Waller?

MRS SCHOEN. She's of absolutely no help of course. The woman's a gawker. As soon as I'm home I'll send you a girl.

SARAH BONETTA. What does it matter? I'm leaving in a few days anyway.

MRS SCHOEN. I shouldn't have let you choose.

SARAH BONETTA. Mama, I want to teach!

MRS SCHOEN. We have already discussed it, Sarah.

SARAH BONETTA *starts to cough.*

To bring all this up in front of that sort / of stranger.

SARAH BONETTA. When else am I meant to bring it up?

MRS SCHOEN. Tincture!

SARAH BONETTA. If she had a few more days, Mama, she would have been perfect.

MRS SCHOEN. Really? Because on more than one occasion you let the conversation go flat and all your guests have disappeared.

SARAH BONETTA. They're not my guests, Mama. I never have the liberty.

SARAH BONETTA *takes the tincture but it doesn't work. Eventually, she will calm down naturally.*

MRS SCHOEN. I never raised you to be conceited.

SARAH BONETTA. All I wanted was for you to present my request to teach etiquette to the Queen. It's nothing considering all that I could / impart to –

MRS SCHOEN. She is the one sending you there to recuperate, not I. Besides, in her current state of thinking I don't think –

SARAH BONETTA. I don't love him, Mama! I have tried. How hard I have tried! You said, Mrs Phipps said, everyone said that love would come. It was only Alice who said otherwise and the otherwise is what is true. I'm not complaining. I'm not. I appreciate how fortunate my situation is.

SARAH BONETTA *finds the salts.* MRS SCHOEN *puts the smelling salts under* AGGIE*'s nose.* AGGIE *comes to. She looks about, disoriented.*

If I am to go to Africa with him, leave my home and everything I love, let me have this one thing. Please?

MRS SCHOEN (*to* AGGIE). You fainted, my dear.

AGGIE *bursts into tears*.

AGGIE. I'm sorry, ma'am.

MRS SCHOEN. Please don't fret.

AGGIE. I've got the sack, haven't I?

SARAH BONETTA. No, you haven't, Aggie.

AGGIE. Then Mr Davies is gonna put me in one of those trunks you got upstairs and ship me off to Africa where them savages with no necks and draggin' arms will boil my head and eat my brains with a pinch of salt and pilchards. That's what One-eyed Ned says he'll do if I ain't any good and that's why Martha left.

MRS SCHOEN. Who's One-eyed Ned?

SARAH BONETTA. The milkman. She gets the butter off him. Mr Davies will do no such thing, Aggie. He's a good, kind man.

MRS SCHOEN. This Ned. Has he been to Africa?

SARAH BONETTA. I don't think he's ever ventured outside the county.

SARAH BONETTA *and* MRS SCHOEN *sit* AGGIE *on the settee.* MRS SCHOEN *makes her a cup of tea with lots of sugar.*

Mama?

MRS SCHOEN *offers* AGGIE *the cup of tea*.

AGGIE. I'm right as, ma'am.

MRS SCHOEN. No you're not.

AGGIE *reluctantly takes the cup*. SARAH BONETTA *offers her the curate stand*.

AGGIE. Ain't I meant to have a side plate?

A beat.

SARAH BONETTA. Yes. Yes, of course.

AGGIE *takes a side plate and puts a piece of cake onto it.*
SARAH BONETTA *and* MRS SCHOEN *observe her taking
a dainty bite before replacing the cake on the side plate.
She chews, takes another bite, replaces the cake on the
side plate.*

MRS WALLER *enters.*

MRS WALLER. Well, they are nowhere to be [seen] – Oh,
she's recovered.

AGGIE *goes to get up.*

MRS SCHOEN. You stay there and finish your tea. (*To* MRS
WALLER.) Yes, she has.

AGGIE *sits back down.*

MRS WALLER. Well that's just splendid. (*To* AGGIE.) You
gave us all quite a fright.

A pause.

SARAH BONETTA. Would you like some more tea, Mrs
Waller?

MRS WALLER. Yes. Thank you.

SARAH BONETTA *rinses out all the cups with the water
and pours the swill into the slop bowl.*

She adds the tea.

Is this really a regular occurrence?

SARAH BONETTA. Yes.

MRS WALLER. Well you must inform a special constable.

SARAH BONETTA. We have. Several times.

MRS SCHOEN. I'll put these things away.

SARAH BONETTA *sits as* MRS SCHOEN *exits. There is
a long silence.* MRS WALLER *watches* AGGIE *as she helps
herself to some Madeira cake.* MRS WALLER *eats straight
from the curate stand rather than taking a side plate.*

MRS WALLER. Well!

A pause.

Etiquette. It really is quite interesting. It's more about habit, breeding, isn't it, rather than something that can simply be taught?

SARAH BONETTA. I disagree.

MRS WALLER. Yes, yes. Of course.

A pause.

I don't envy your decision what not to take to Africa. What will you do with what you leave behind?

SARAH BONETTA. I'll put it in storage for when I return.

MRS WALLER. Oh, you want to return?

SARAH BONETTA. Yes. Of course. Eventually.

MRS WALLER *picks up the painting that* SARAH BONETTA *picked up earlier on.*

MRS WALLER. Is this a Constable?

SARAH BONETTA. Yes, it is.

MRS WALLER. You really are quite fortunate.

Silence.

Did you manage to catch those Ethiopian entertainers when they came to London?

SARAH BONETTA. No, I'm afraid not.

MRS WALLER. They were jolly good. I was quite ignorant as to what to expect. I was expecting the usual drumming and trumpet playing but, surprisingly, they were physical performers. Let's just say they do some very entertaining tricks with their limbs. It was quite shocking. I believe they are going to be in Southampton in the next couple of days so you might be able to see them there. I really do recommend them before you leave.

Silence.

AGGIE. I think it might rain.

MRS WALLER. I'm sorry?

AGGIE. Rain. I think it might. But it's such good weather for September. Last week the weather was just miserable. Drizzle the entire day. I don't like drizzle.

SARAH BONETTA. It's terrible, isn't it?

AGGIE. Yes, Mrs Davies. It really is.

ACT TWO

A Household, Cheshire, present day

SARAH *is on the phone. In front of* SARAH, *there is a partially eaten slice of cake and a cup of tea.* JAMES *enters partway through the conversation and observes her.*

JAMES *has a black eye and his arm in a sling. This sits incongruously with his smart attire.*

SARAH. Of course. Of course. Of course. It's exactly what I've been wanting to sink my teeth into... I'm excited. I'm incredibly excited... I am so excited. Really. You really need to see my face to see just how excited I am. No, I have never been before... I am... That's right. Originally. Yes. My parents were born there... Well, I haven't had any real desire to go. Really. I thought I mentioned that before, Andy. Several times. There are just so many other countries that I prefer. Like Hong Kong, Malaysia. The whole of Southeast Asia. But I'm excited to be going now. Incredibly excited. Although I thought Rich Webb would have been your first choice... But I'm excited. God I'm excited. All that culture... Yes, it will be an experience. I had a feeling that's what you were going to say. Okay. Great. Great. I'll talk to Maria on Monday... You too. Thanks, Andy, have a great weekend.

SARAH *hangs up and immediately smooshes the cake. She realises* JAMES *is watching her.*

Andy Head.

JAMES. Yes, I / [gathered].

SARAH. I'm going.

JAMES. Yes, I –

SARAH. Tom Gannon really should be the one to go. Or Rich Webb. I said to him I was surprised Rich wasn't his first choice.

JAMES. Oh – [right].

SARAH. Do you know what he said?

JAMES. No. What did / he – ?

SARAH. Not that I can't project manage this. Of course I can manage this. You know I can.

JAMES. Of course / [you] –

SARAH. I told him I could.

JAMES. What?

SARAH. Project manage it.

JAMES. Good.

SARAH. Though we all said we'd prefer not to go. In the group meeting. I told you that, right? About the group meeting?

JAMES. Yes I think you / [did].

SARAH. We were all asked about it. About going. We all said it. That we'd rather not. Although thinking about it, maybe I should've been more assertive.

JAMES. What's more assertive than saying you'd rather not? And if you all said you'd rather / not –

SARAH. The thing is, he was acting like he really wanted the gig. It should be his gig.

JAMES. Who was?

SARAH. Rich Webb. He was part of the tender offer. Even met the Transport Minister. They bonded, they said. All three of them. He took pains to tell us how much they'd all bonded.

JAMES. Who did? Rich?

SARAH. No, Andrew Head. Laughing about it with that same laugh and how the only reason the Minister accepted their tender was because Rich threw in a pair of Arsenal tickets which were negotiated up to season tickets and how ingenious it all was because up until then the Chinese had it in the bag. Course I don't believe it.

JAMES. Believe what? That the Minister would accept a bribe?

SARAH. Of course he'd accept a bribe. The story. They probably said it to make the whole thing more interesting. That's what they do. Talk things up. Our meetings consist of who can tell the most interesting anecdote. I can tell anecdotes too, you know. I mean, the one about Belize and the scorpions is funny. I can make people laugh. I can be funny.

JAMES. Well –

SARAH. I'm hilarious.

JAMES. You are.

SARAH. But I'm not going to shout above everyone else to be heard only to have him talk over me with an overinflated anecdote.

JAMES. Who will? Rich Webb?

SARAH. Yes, of course, Rich Webb. Who else have I been talking about? He really should be the one to go.

JAMES. Well, of course he should go.

SARAH. Why?

A beat.

JAMES. Well, because he's more…

SARAH. He's more experienced.

JAMES. Exactly.

SARAH. It's because I don't network enough. If I networked more it would be better. I would be better. Because I do a great job.

JAMES. You / [do] –

SARAH. And go to the pub. I should've gone to the pub. And laugh at their jokes more. Tried to be more – Although it doesn't matter what I do cos they'll never forget the shoe incident.

JAMES. That was four years ago.

SARAH. I shouldn't have thrown it. Lost my temper.

JAMES. That temp was incompetent.

SARAH. They still call me Naomi Campbell behind my back.
    It's fine. It's fine. There are more civilised ways of dealing
    with it.

JAMES. Yes.

SARAH *looks at him*.

There are more… It was a really difficult time.

SARAH. It *was* a difficult time. Petra had just died. It's fine.
    It'll be fine. I don't know. Maybe I should just leave. But if
    I leave they'll think I'm not up to it. But they never give me
    credit for my ideas anyway. And if I say something – But
    it'll be the same if I go somewhere else. I'll have to start
    again. It'll be the same people just different faces.

Silence.

JAMES. Maybe / [if you] –

SARAH. You want to know what the real reason is, right? Why
    Rich isn't going?

JAMES. Why?

SARAH. His wife doesn't trust him.

JAMES. Okay.

SARAH. He cheated on her in Thailand with three Thai girls so
    all exotic places are out which is ridiculous because it's only
    Asians he likes so there isn't really a problem.

JAMES. I don't remember Rich's partner being Asian.

SARAH. She isn't. And it doesn't help that Maria fancies him
    rotten so probably pushed the sympathy vote even further.

JAMES. Sympathy for – ?

SARAH. Him getting caught with the Asian girls.

JAMES. Right. But isn't Maria just the secretary?

SARAH. She isn't *just* the secretary. She's Andrew Head's secretary.

JAMES. Right. So what about Tom Gannon? Why isn't he – ?

SARAH. Maria fancies him as well so she would have
    championed his cause.

JAMES. So, what I understand is you've got the worst project to manage because –

SARAH. Maria doesn't fancy me.

JAMES. Right. So it's got nothing to do with Andrew Head?

SARAH. It's got everything to do with Andrew Head. But she doesn't help. She loathes me. But it's fine. I told you about the flights, right? How she's never able to change my flights but always manages to change theirs?

JAMES. Yes. / You –

SARAH. Says it's too complicated. I changed my flight once. Tom and Rich change theirs all the time but all they need to do is feed her a banal compliment – Have you changed your hair, Maria? And she's practically wetting her chair. Clearly she sees me as some sort of threat but I keep reminding her: I am a friend. Although she would see a sign for the women's toilets competition she is that insecure. She's the worst type of woman. Needs to feel like she's the only woman in the room. They drew lots, apparently. That's what he told me. Johnathan Carney. I cornered him yesterday – we were on the same Tube. He's okay, Johnathan Carney. New. Sweet. The only one who gives me real eye contact. They were in the pub and drew lots. It was the night Victoria was sick.

JAMES. But that was / [weeks ago] –

SARAH. Weeks ago. I know. Said Rich Webb drew on my behalf. I said, that was a coincidence that I got the short straw as I was absent. He said, yes. But the way he said it was strange. So I said, in a jokey, light, sort of way, I bet you didn't really draw lots. I bet it was just a flat-out vote. He hesitated. Went red. Insisted they drew lots. Said I was being paranoid but if he wasn't acting suspicious he wouldn't have gone red.

JAMES. Why would they draw lots if they knew they weren't going to Nigeria anyway?

SARAH. Because they have to at least pretend to be democratic. Or I could be being paranoid. Maybe I am being paranoid? Maybe Johnathan Carney's right.

JAMES. He's not right.

SARAH. I just feel there's no one there I can trust.

JAMES. What about your friend / Ruth?

SARAH. Ruth? Ruth's not a friend any more. Not after she got drunk at the Christmas party, did the box splits in the middle of the dance floor in front of Andy Head and got the Bergamo gig. Up until then I thought I was getting it. She even said it. 'I'll put a good word in for you.'

JAMES. You are amazing. Talented. Cleverer than all of them.

SARAH. I am amazing, talented and cleverer than all of them.

They kiss tenderly.

I still feel like shit. I just have to work harder.

The doorbell goes. JAMES *goes to answer.*

JAMES. Your talent will shine through in the end.

SARAH. Whoever it is, tell them we don't want any.

JAMES. And look on the bright side.

SARAH. What bright side?

JAMES. It'll be two years away from them.

SARAH heads for the kitchen with her smooshed cake.

And it can't be that bad if the Chinese can hack it. And it's a great thing to have on your CV. Not as great as Southeast Asia, obviously.

JAMES answers the door to HARRIET and BEN. HARRIET is the pleasing type, eager to laugh, clearly highly strung. BEN is more reserved. He has a local accent.

HARRIET. Hi! You must be James. Harriet. This is my husband, Ben.

BEN. Hi.

HARRIET. From number nine.

JAMES. Oh right. Right.

HARRIET. Louisa's friends.

JAMES. Right. (*Calling*.) Sarah! It's Harriet and Ben! Louisa's friends. From number nine.

SARAH approaches. She still holds her plate of smooshed cake.

SARAH. Ben, Harriet, hi.

HARRIET/BEN. Hi.

A beat.

HARRIET. We wanted to see how you were settling in.

SARAH. Thank you. That's really kind of you.

JAMES. And we are.

HARRIET and BEN look confused.

Settling in.

They laugh. There is a bit of an uncomfortable silence. HARRIET presents them with a basket of muffins.

HARRIET. Gluten-free muffins.

SARAH. Thank you. That's very kind of you.

HARRIET. I thought best to be on the safe side. You have no idea how much of a discussion we had. You can't just assume. Not nowadays.

A beat.

Gluten.

SARAH. Right.

HARRIET. Make something with nuts and you've got someone in an anaphylactic shock. And don't get me started on soy.

JAMES. Yes, soy! Terrible.

HARRIET. So are you – [gluten intolerant]?

SARAH. No. No. We're not.

JAMES. Just lactose.

HARRIET. Sorry?

JAMES. Intolerant.

HARRIET. I knew we should have gone with the flapjacks!

SARAH. It's / fine.

HARRIET. No. It's not. I should've checked with Louisa first.

BEN. She says it's fine.

SARAH. Really.

HARRIET. Not a problem.

SARAH. It's fine.

HARRIET. I can whip up a few in about an hour or so although the oats won't be organic.

SARAH. James is joking. That was a joke.

HARRIET. Oh. Right.

A beat.

They laugh.

So you do both eat dairy?

SARAH. Yes we do.

SARAH *takes the basket from* HARRIET.

Thank you.

An uncomfortable silence.

JAMES. Would you like a cup of tea? Or – ?

HARRIET. If it's all right?

JAMES. Of course it is.

HARRIET. We don't want to intrude.

BEN. Unless you're busy of course.

SARAH. You're not intruding.

JAMES. Any friend of Louisa's –

SARAH. And we should say thank you for the welcome basket of fantastic-looking muffins. They smell fantastic.

HARRIET. Well, if you insist.

JAMES. We do.

A pause.

SARAH. Well, you'd better come in.

HARRIET *and* BEN *enter.*

JAMES. So you're friends of Louisa?

HARRIET. Yes. We've known her for – How long have we known her?

BEN. Since we moved here. So twelve / years.

HARRIET. Twelve years.

A pause.

Have you been getting her updates?

JAMES. Yes.

HARRIET. They're terrific, aren't they?

BEN. Lucky for some.

A pause.

SARAH. So is it coffee or tea? The coffee's freshly ground.

HARRIET. Tea. Herbal. We've both given up caffeine. We're trying to manage the day without artificial stimulants. There's a TED Talk about it. Have you seen it?

SARAH. No.

HARRIET. A twenty-minute jog every morning is all you need to get the same benefit as your morning fix.

BEN. Apparently. I'm still waiting for it to kick in.

They laugh.

HARRIET. Anyway…

An uncomfortable beat.

Tea for us.

JAMES. Tea it is.

BEN. Unless you don't have any herbal?

SARAH. Yes we do.

BEN. Course you do.

HARRIET. Terrific.

JAMES. Sarah's a herbal fiend.

HARRIET. Great. So am I.

A pause.

I hope you like them.

SARAH. I'm sure we will. They smell fantastic.

BEN. Harriet's quite the pastry chef.

HARRIET. Ben, it's never appropriate to start a conversation with people you don't know with: 'Harriet's quite the pastry chef.'

JAMES. Of course it's appropriate if you are.

BEN. And I didn't start the / conversation with it.

HARRIET. It sounds like we're fishing, which we're not. It's because I won a baking programme.

JAMES. What baking programme?

A pause.

Oh. Right.

HARRIET. I don't like to go on about it.

BEN. We have a superstar in our midst.

HARRIET. Please don't.

JAMES. Do people recognise you in the street?

HARRIET. No. No. Okay, yes maybe sometimes. It's so embarrassing. Really. I just wish he'd stop going on about it.

BEN. If a husband can't crow about his wife's achievements... I bet you crow about your wife's achievements.

JAMES. Yes, I do.

BEN. There you go.

HARRIET. And I didn't win. I was runner-up. Which makes it even more embarrassing because he always tells people I won.

BEN. Everyone loves her lemon drizzle cake.

HARRIET. Moving swiftly on.

JAMES. Coincidentally, we just bought a lemon drizzle cake from the local bakery. Lovely little shop.

BEN. Harriet's by any chance?

A beat.

The lemon drizzle is her best-seller.

BEN *and* HARRIET *notice* SARAH*'s plate with the squished cake.*

SARAH. It was lovely. It really was.

JAMES. My wife had a bit of bad news.

BEN. So the cake got it in the neck?

SARAH. Something like that. Yes.

They laugh. Another uncomfortable silence.

JAMES (*to* SARAH). So tea?

SARAH. Yes.

HARRIET. If it's not too much bother.

SARAH. Great.

SARAH *exits to the kitchen.* JAMES, HARRIET *and* BEN *make themselves comfortable.*

HARRIET. What wonderful chairs!

JAMES. Thank you.

HARRIET. Brightens up the place. Not that Louisa's house is dull. It's great. It really is. But it's nice to have your own things even if the house is already furnished.

JAMES. Right.

BEN. So you've settled in all right, then?

JAMES. Well enough.

BEN. Great.

HARRIET. Great.

BEN. Great.

There's a short silence.

HARRIET. We've lived here for twelve years. I've said that already, haven't I?

BEN. Yes.

HARRIET. It's all right. The street. Quiet. Not as lively as London, I imagine. But the people here are really decent. Friendly. Maybe a little set in their ways. But on the whole, they're good. They look out for one another. That sort of thing, which can be good. You know. We have a very low burglary rate.

A pause.

How about London? Are the neighbours – ?

JAMES. No. We all keep ourselves to ourselves most of the time.

HARRIET. That can be good too.

JAMES. It has its advantages.

BEN. Where were you living in London? I think Louisa did say.

JAMES. Chelsea.

BEN. Swish.

JAMES. You know London at all?

HARRIET. We've been there a couple of times, haven't we? We have friends there. They live in Wandsworth. Do you know Wandsworth?

JAMES. I've driven through it.

HARRIET. It's all right. You know, lots to do. We went out in Clapham.

JAMES. Clapham's very nice.

A pause.

HARRIET. I really like these chairs.

JAMES. Thank you. I upholstered them myself.

HARRIET. Amazing. Ben, aren't they amazing?

BEN. Yes. They look great, mate.

A pause.

JAMES. So a bakery!

HARRIET. Well, a patisserie. It's always been a dream of mine.

JAMES. Nice. The programme must've been good publicity?

HARRIET. I suppose it was.

A long silence.

BEN. Cambodia. That's where she is. Right now. That's what it said on Facebook. Siem Reap.

JAMES. Cambodia. Great place.

BEN. You've been?

JAMES. Yes.

A pause.

HARRIET. Guyana sounds exciting, too. That's where she said you've just come from. In her email.

JAMES. Yes.

HARRIET. All that sun.

BEN. You must be feeling it, mate. The change in weather.

HARRIET. It's been pretty warm here recently, though, hasn't it?

BEN. Yes. For Cheshire.

HARRIET. You must've brought the warm weather with you.

BEN. Enjoy it while you can.

A pause.

HARRIET. We've always wanted to go to the West Indies, haven't we? Hop around the islands. Jamaica... Barbados... Guyana.

JAMES. It's in South America. Guyana. Between Suriname and Venezuela.

HARRIET. Oh right. I'm sorry. I should've known that.

BEN. Well, that's something to put away for the pub quiz.

HARRIET. You must join us for the quiz. It's every second Wednesday in The Hare and Hound, which is just by the Sainsbury's Local. We always need members.

BEN. If you like pub quizzes, that is.

HARRIET. Do you?

JAMES. On occasion.

HARRIET. Great well, we'll sign you up.

JAMES. Great.

Silence.

So you're a pastry chef and you are – ?

BEN. An accountant. Moving swiftly on.

They laugh.

HARRIET. What do you do?

JAMES. I'm an amateur boxer. In case you were wondering where I got this.

HARRIET. No. We weren't / wondering, were we?

BEN. You got that from / boxing?

HARRIET. I mean, we were because, I mean, you can't help but notice.

JAMES. It's in your face, right?

HARRIET. Yes it really is.

A pause.

BEN. Boxing?

JAMES. Yes. You should see the other guy.

This time, HARRIET *and* BEN *do not laugh.*

In my other life, I'm a university professor. Nineteenth-century history. I also buy and sell antiques in my spare time. That's my real interest.

HARRIET. That sounds really exciting, doesn't it, Ben?

BEN. Yeah.

JAMES. Not as exciting as having your own bakery.

HARRIET. Well, it's really a patisserie.

Silence.

BEN. So what do you deal in, mate?

JAMES. Furniture, silverware, letters, books.

SARAH *enters with a tea tray. On it is a selection box of teas, cups. Hot water.*

SARAH. So, I have a selection.

HARRIET. Great.

BEN. Great.

JAMES. Great.

HARRIET *examines the box of teas.*

HARRIET. What a brilliant idea. It's rather like a hotel.

SARAH. I can't take the praise. It's Louisa's. We haven't had time to fill the kitchen.

HARRIET. I was just saying there's a Sainsbury's just by the roundabout.

SARAH. Yes. We've seen it. Thank you.

HARRIET. No problemo.

They choose.

Sicilian lemongrass sounds good.

BEN. I'll have a jasmine green tea.

HARRIET *and* BEN *help themselves to teabags and put them in the cups of water.*

SARAH. So what did I miss?

JAMES. I was telling them how I got my injuries. Boxing.

HARRIET. He really has got a weird sense of humour.

JAMES. Went down like a lead balloon.

SARAH. So what do you think happened then? If you think he was joking?

Silence.

HARRIET. Well, we didn't think...

BEN *and* HARRIET *exchange uncomfortable glances.*

We heard something, didn't we, Ben? From the neighbours. And I want... We want... We want to say it shouldn't have happened, don't we? It was wrong. Bang out of order. What the police did. That's all we wanted to say.

Silence.

SARAH. Well, that's very much appreciated.

A pause.

JAMES. I was telling them about antique dealing.

HARRIET. Yes. Yes. He was. And it just sounds so interesting. I mean, these chairs...

BEN. What's your most lucrative find?

HARRIET. Ben! You don't have to say.

JAMES. A letter from Queen Victoria.

HARRIET. Wow.

BEN. That's brilliant, mate.

JAMES. Well, it's still being authenticated.

BEN. Really? Who authenticates it?

JAMES. The Royal Family.

BEN. How did you find it?

JAMES. eBay, actually. It was with some other letters in an out-of-print book. Funny story, actually. Don't know if it's true but the bloke who sold them to me in Croydon – that's where he was from – tells me this story. He tells me he's getting rid of some junk, right? We're in his grandmother's house he'd inherited. He shows me all this junk, which isn't really junk at all, it's books and paintings – not anything expensive but, you know, nice, all hoarded by his grandmother from her grandmother's grandmother, so his great-great-great-great-grandmother, you get my drift, who apparently, now, here's where it's interesting, was a madwoman who pretended to be rich and managed to inveigle her way into the highest echelons of society so that she could stalk royalty. She stole heaps of stuff from them.

BEN. You're having a laugh.

JAMES. That's the story.

HARRIET. What was her name?

JAMES. Harriet Waller.

BEN (*amused*). Harriet.

JAMES. Apparently no one noticed she was off her trolley for years.

HARRIET. How could they not notice?

BEN. She's upper-class. Mad means eccentric.

JAMES. Precise/ly.

HARRIET. You don't say mad, Ben. You say mentally impaired.

SARAH cuts up the cake and gives them all a slice.
HARRIET and BEN watch JAMES and SARAH take a bite.

JAMES. It's gorgeous.

SARAH. Gorgeous.

JAMES. It really is.

HARRIET. Not too much lemon?

SARAH. No.

HARRIET. Great.

They eat.

So who was the recipient? Of the letter?

JAMES. A woman called Sarah Bonetta. She was an African in the royal circles. There were also letters from Princess Alice, one of Queen Victoria's children.

BEN. Must be worth a mint.

HARRIET. Ben!

JAMES. I haven't actually had them valued. Right now, I'm using them as source material for a historical novel. What Princess Alice tells Bonetta in her letters is pure dynamite.

HARRIET. Like what?

JAMES. You'll have to wait for the book.

They laugh.

BEN. I can't believe this bloke had no idea he was sitting on a gold mine?

SARAH. It was stolen property anyway.

HARRIET. But it's all so interesting. The letters… the African lady. She sounds really interesting. I mean, who was she?

JAMES. All we know is that she was an orphan given as a gift to Queen Victoria when she was seven. For an African, she was considered highly intelligent by their standards.

HARRIET. Given?

JAMES. Apparently. By an African king. Under Queen Victoria she lived a regal life. Died of tuberculosis.

HARRIET. That's a story.

BEN. But she was generous like that, wasn't she? That's what you hear. I mean, she had that bloke from India.

JAMES. Abdul.

HARRIET. To be given to someone as a gift. I just can't imagine it.

BEN. Don't think she would have had any complaints. Slavery or royalty?

HARRIET. It's still barbaric. I suppose it was all barbaric back then.

SARAH. They still are barbaric.

HARRIET. I didn't mean just Africa.

SARAH. I do. Parts of it, anyway. Completely corrupt. Backwards I'd say.

HARRIET. Don't you think maybe those countries simply get a lot of bad press?

SARAH. What, like the kidnappings, the raping and murdering of innocent kids or the general corruption?

HARRIET. Everywhere's corrupt if you dig deep enough. Look at America and the elections.

SARAH. Some places are worse than others. I just think everything about, let's say Nigeria, is shit.

HARRIET. I don't know. I mean, I wouldn't expect a country which has probably been oppressed for years by the British, to run like clockwork.

SARAH. You're right. I'd at least expect it to run.

A pause.

JAMES. The food's good, though. We love the food. Been to a few good restaurants.

BEN. We're not as adventurous. Although we've got an Albanian restaurant in the village. Haven't tried it. We like Japanese.

JAMES. Love Japanese food.

BEN. Yes.

A silence.

Spain.

A beat.

My favourite country. I know it's not exactly the Tropics.

JAMES. Spain is underrated.

BEN. You get the heat but there's also familiarity.

JAMES. Always a safe bet.

A pause.

BEN. Australia. Next.

A beat.

Louisa. Apparently.

HARRIET. Yes. Australia.

JAMES. Australia.

BEN. I think it's a midlife crisis if you ask me. Off to find herself at forty.

JAMES. What did you do when you turned forty?

BEN. Not much. (*To* HARRIET.) You applied to *Bake Off*, didn't you?

HARRIET. The neighbours applied for me. I didn't have a clue till the interview. You ran the London Marathon.

BEN. Oh yeah. Raised two grand for Oxfam. Before, you know, the scandal.

A pause.

SARAH. I'm going to check on Victoria. If you'll excuse me.

HARRIET. Yes, of course.

SARAH *exits*.

JAMES. Victoria's our daughter. But you already know that –

HARRIET. Yes.

JAMES. Because of the neighbours.

HARRIET. Yes.

A pause.

BEN. So Sarah's a structural engineer.

JAMES. Yes, she is.

BEN. Can't imagine there are too many women in the field. Or many, you know –

JAMES. There aren't.

BEN. I don't think I know any structural engineers. Or even engineers.

HARRIET. I find that you need to be more than just good at your job these days to get on. On *Bake Off* I felt that there had to be a type. The sexy one, the ditzy one. That sort of thing.

JAMES. Which one were you?

HARRIET. I fell partway between the grandma-everyone-loves and sexy-mum-of-two. My point is, since when has work become a personality contest? It should be just about the talent.

BEN. Has she built anything interesting?

JAMES. Bridges… Roads… Hospitals… Office blocks…

BEN. It's like leaving a legacy.

HARRIET. Must be hard, though.

JAMES. We manage. I'm the househusband.

BEN. Rather you than me.

HARRIET. Ben!

BEN. You know I'd do anything for the boys but I wouldn't want to be with them twenty-four hours a day.

JAMES. Sarah's the same.

BEN. I don't think they've suffered for it. My absence.

HARRIET. Let's wait until they're in their twenties.

A pause.

Is she adopted then? Your little girl?

JAMES. No. We bought her from white slave traders.

A short burst of laughter.

HARRIET. You're joking.

JAMES. You're catching on. Of course she's adopted.

HARRIET. I hope it's okay to ask? I don't have a problem with it.

JAMES. It's fine. We're asked that question all the time.

HARRIET. Even in London?

JAMES. Always in London. We get loads of misunderstandings in London.

HARRIET. That's such a relief to know. For the neighbours. I know they're feeling really bad about it all.

SARAH *enters with some hot water.*

SARAH. Top-up, anyone?

HARRIET. Yes, please.

BEN. Please.

SARAH *tops up* HARRIET *and* BEN*'s cups, eats more of her cake.*

SARAH. This is just divine, Harriet.

HARRIET. Lemon rind. That's what gives it that extra zing.

JAMES. Harriet and Ben were just saying how bad the neighbours feel about the incident.

SARAH. Which ones? The ones who called the police or all of them?

HARRIET. The ones who called the police.

SARAH. You should tell them to come round. Tell them we don't bite.

HARRIET. Yes, we will.

A pause.

James was saying you get a lot of misunderstandings. You know about –

SARAH. Yes. The number of occasions people ask me how much I charge.

HARRIET *and* BEN *look blank.*

For being a nanny. Do nannies wear Prada? I say.

They laugh.

HARRIET. I just want to say, I don't have a problem with it. I think it's fantastic you've adopted a child from a different race. We have friends who are adopting. They'd adopt any race, of course. But they're worried about the child fitting in. Not that yours doesn't. But I suppose they've got their own reasons for not – They say they could get a baby the race they want but it'll probably be damaged. Not that there's anything wrong with a damaged child. It's not the child's fault, is it? Anyway, I was wondering if maybe you could talk to them about how you managed to adopt a child of a different race. That wasn't damaged or… I hate using the word damaged. I'm sorry, I don't even know if she's – There has to be a better word.

JAMES. Her mother wasn't addicted to crack if that's what you mean.

HARRIET. Yes. No. Not that I wouldn't – I would. We would. If we had room, wouldn't we?

BEN. What? Adopt a crack-child?

HARRIET. No. Yes. Look, I've got nothing against crack… the babies, I mean. Anyway, if there was a specific agency you could recommend.

SARAH. Not really. Ours was a private adoption.

HARRIET. Oh right.

A beat.

So what does that entail, exactly?

SARAH. Victoria's birth mother was a good friend of mine. She died when Victoria was eight months. Ovarian cancer.

HARRIET. Oh my God, that's just so – I'm sorry. That must have been awful.

SARAH. Yes it was.

HARRIET. And there wasn't any other family?

SARAH. There was. Complete shits.

A pause.

HARRIET. That's just great that she entrusted her child to people who she thought would do the best job.

SARAH. We think so.

JAMES. As soon as we held her she felt like she was ours.

HARRIET. That's just great. It really is.

A pause.

And she doesn't ask about her real family or think – ?

SARAH. Yes, of course she asks.

HARRIET. I'm sorry if this is too –

SARAH. It's fine. We get these questions all the time.

HARRIET. It's because it's so rare, isn't it? You know, this way around.

SARAH. We know.

A pause.

HARRIET. I mean, I don't think you could do it, you know, this way around if you went through the system.

SARAH. I don't know.

HARRIET. I don't think you can because there's such a demand out there for white babies. Well, that's what my friends say.

SARAH. Like I said, I really don't know. We went privately. Privately you can adopt any colour of the rainbow.

A pause.

HARRIET. Well, I think it's great.

Awkward silence.

BEN. My line manager has a Chinese girl. Adopted. He's white. No one bats an eyelid.

HARRIET. East Asian.

BEN. Sorry?

HARRIET. East Asian. You don't know if they're Chinese.

BEN. She looks Chinese.

HARRIET. You can't really tell by their look, Ben.

BEN. I think you can. It's subtle. But you can. Well I can.

HARRIET. Well, not everyone can. So it's East Asian for ease.

BEN. Somehow I don't think it's the Chinese who are struggling with what they call themselves.

HARRIET. Think you'll find that's what they're calling themselves. Not the Chinese in China obviously. People are proud of their identities, Ben.

BEN. Is that what the app says?

JAMES. There's an app?

BEN. Of course there's an app. There's an app for everything.

HARRIET. I just like being considerate.

BEN. Because everyone's offended by the slightest thing.

HARRIET. I'm sorry.

SARAH. I know what you mean.

HARRIET. We debate about this constantly.

SARAH. It's like when did the word fat become a profanity?

BEN. Yes! You're fat. Yes. It's a description. A fact. Like the fact you have hands. A head. You're fat. You're small.

HARRIET. You can't say small.

BEN. Vertically challenged.

HARRIET. But if vertically challenged people find the word offensive.

BEN. Someone at work the other day said we couldn't use the word brainstorm.

SARAH. Why can't you say brainstorm?

BEN. Because we might offend epileptics. There weren't even any epileptics in the room. It's political correctness gone mad.

HARRIET. It's not. (*To* SARAH *and* JAMES.) I'm sorry but you would hate it if people called you, I'm sorry, black, instead of bame, wouldn't you?

SARAH. Bame?

HARRIET. B-A-M-E. Or is it bamé. I've seen it once with an accent. It means 'Black and ethnic minority'.

SARAH. Oh it's an acronym.

JAMES. Then it should be B-A-E-M.

HARRIET. So it's not bamé?

SARAH. Are we meant to be spelling it or saying it?

HARRIET. You really haven't heard of it?

SARAH. No.

JAMES. I have. It's creeping in at work. There they say bammy.

BEN. I think that's offensive. Don't you think that's offensive?

HARRIET. No, Ben. It's how you put a person at ease –

BEN. By calling her a name she doesn't like or hasn't even heard of? She, *they* are being corralled into one group that's basically called non-white.

HARRIET. BAME doesn't mean non-white.

BEN. Of course it means non-white! What else does it mean? There's white and there's everyone else with a name that no one can say properly. Or even knows how to say. That's offensive.

HARRIET. You're saying being non-white is a negative.

BEN. Course it is. It's being defined by what you're not. I'm right, right?

JAMES. Well –

BEN. Hello, I'm Ben, I'm not rich. Hello, I'm Ben, I'm not attractive. It's all a load of bollocks. They agree, don't you, mate?

SARAH. BAME. What does it even mean?

HARRIET. It's a BAME person. Or bamé.

JAMES. Or / bammy.

HARRIET. And it's not about offending.

BEN. Person! Would you call yourself a BAME person, Sarah?

SARAH. No. I wouldn't call myself a BAME person.

BEN. Because it's offensive. Racist. That's racist.

SARAH. I would call myself a white person.

Silence.

BEN. Sorry?

SARAH. I would call myself a white person. Well, culturally white.

Silence.

BEN *laughs out loud.*

HARRIET. Ben!

BEN. You're... Is this a southern thing?

SARAH. I believe that being black or white is more than just skin colour. I mean that's non-negotiable but everything around it is.

A pause.

James and I identify more with the English culture. All our influences are white. Our friends, music, food –

BEN. What's culturally white food nowadays?

JAMES. Bangers and mash and toad in the hole.

BEN. I don't know anyone who eats toad in the hole.

JAMES. Fish and chips then.

BEN. Black people don't eat fish and chips? Come on.

HARRIET. Ben –

JAMES. Not as much as chicken. I mean that's a black thing. Eating a lot of chicken.

HARRIET. I'm not sure that's true.

JAMES. We're pescatarians, by the way.

SARAH. Our influences, our taste in music and dress, food, language. They're all white.

BEN. But your parents are black.

SARAH. James was adopted by white parents and there weren't any black people where I grew up. I'm not close to my family. Never felt like I fitted in. We really don't know any other black people.

Silence.

BEN. Okay. I'm sorry if I was – It's just it's the first time I've heard of this.

HARRIET. I get it completely. It's just like how I don't ever see colour. I just see people.

BEN. If you can see he's wearing a red jumper you can see his black face.

HARRIET. What I mean is we're all the same underneath. I treat people all the same. And it makes complete sense you wanting to adopt a white baby if that's how you feel.

A pause.

BEN. Well I really find it hard to believe that you don't know any black people.

SARAH. Why?

HARRIET. Yes, why, Ben? Do we?

BEN. Yes.

HARRIET. Who?

BEN. My friend from work. Sam.

HARRIET. Sam's not a friend, Ben. He's a colleague.

BEN. But I know him. And we live in Cheshire. If we lived in London.

SARAH. It's really not something we'd lie about.

BEN. I'm not accusing you of lying, mate. I just find it –

SARAH. Incomprehensible.

HARRIET. Everyone has a right to feel black white gay straight or whatever, Ben. It's not about the packaging, like I said.

BEN. Sure. Fine. Great.

HARRIET. I'm sorry about my husband. He's just not used to diversity. It's not diverse around here. It should be. He finds the whole transgender thing difficult to grasp, too.

BEN. I do. I'm not ashamed to admit it.

SARAH. You do know that just because you can't comprehend it, doesn't mean it doesn't exist. That I can't feel the way I feel.

BEN. You can feel what you feel but I'm also allowed to react in the way I react. It's still a free country.

A pause.

HARRIET. I'm sorry. Maybe we should – ?

JAMES. No. Don't. Please. I feel it would be wrong for you to leave without you understanding us. After all, you came here to do that, right?

HARRIET. We didn't come here to upset anyone.

JAMES. We're not upset. Are you upset?

SARAH. I'm not upset.

JAMES. Ben?

BEN. I'm great.

JAMES. See?

HARRIET. Great.

Silence.

JAMES. Would anyone like another cup of tea?

HARRIET. No thank you.

BEN. No.

JAMES. Sarah?

SARAH. I'm fine.

A long silence.

HARRIET. I was told once that I danced like a BAME woman.

BEN. What?

HARRIET. BAME. A black woman. Black. It was years ago now. I was told I was earthy.

JAMES. And I've been told on countless occasions that I've got the rhythm of a pogo stick.

HARRIET. I think it's changing. We'll all merge into one in the end.

JAMES. Not physically. Black people can't swim.

HARRIET. Of course black people can swim! That's a myth. It's a myth, isn't it?

JAMES. Where were they in the Olympics?

HARRIET. I'm sure they were there. They were there. I know they were there.

JAMES. The running, the boxing.

SARAH. White people have more fat-to-muscle / so they float.

HARRIET. This is silly. I heard it's the hair. Put a baby in the water any colour and they swim but then black people choose not to because of their hair.

SARAH. So is it physical and cultural?

HARRIET. It's just cultural. I'm sure it is.

BEN. Can you swim?

SARAH. Yes.

JAMES. No.

SARAH (*amused, to* JAMES). It looks like you're blacker than you think.

SARAH *and* JAMES *laugh.*

HARRIET. I see more black children in the pools when I go for a swim. Obviously not round here. When I stay with my sister in Maidstone. I just don't think you can distinguish between cultures nowadays. I think it's blurred.

BEN. Course you can.

JAMES. You can.

SARAH. I think you can.

HARRIET *kisses her teeth incredibly loudly. There is a long silence.*

BEN. Where the hell did you learn to do that?

HARRIET. That's what I'm saying. I just think you can't distinguish too much between cultures nowadays.

SARAH. Well, I've felt white all my life.

BEN. But you married a black man!

HARRIET. Who's culturally white.

SARAH. I didn't say I wasn't attracted to black men physically.

HARRIET. People marry different races, Ben. Colour's got nothing to do with it. I get it. I really do. I've always wanted to live somewhere more multicultural.

BEN. Since when?

HARRIET. Since we had the boys. It's your family that's here. Not mine. Mine's in Kent.

JAMES. We feel quite comfortable here.

BEN. You were attacked by the police.

HARRIET. Ben!

JAMES. It's fine.

A pause.

I mean, of course, bad things happen to us because of our skin but it's all about how it affects you. When I was seventeen, a friend and I ditched school and went to the beach in Camber Sands. We were walking along the road, there wasn't a pavement and this white van sped past and someone from inside shouted the n-word. I had no idea who he was talking to. I knew his intention but it didn't process. Didn't sink in. Add up. Compute. The thing is, I was not offended. I actually forgot about it. I believe a culturally black person would be going on and on about it. Blaming everything wrong in their lives on racism when it's usually something else.

SARAH. Do you feel white, Ben?

BEN. Mate, mate, leave me out if it. I don't need to question my –

SARAH. Come on. You're with friends. We're friends now, right? We're the same.

BEN. We're not the same.

SARAH. Why not?

BEN. Somehow I get the impression you're trying to make me say something I don't want to say.

SARAH. I'm not trying to make you say anything, Ben. Unless there's something you feel like you should be saying.

HARRIET. If I was blind I'm not sure I would feel white!

Silence.

I'm sorry, I mean visually impaired.

SARAH. How would you feel?

BEN. Harriet –

HARRIET. I don't know. I don't think it's that straightforward. I'd feel, well, I'd feel blended.

SARAH. Blended?

HARRIET. Yeah, like mixed-race.

BEN. Harriet –

HARRIET. Well, biracial. That's what it's called now. Biracial.

BEN. How do you know what a mixed-race person feels like?

HARRIET. Torn. In whatever I do. Work. Relationships. Not quite myself at times. I mean, who am I really? That's how I imagine they feel.

BEN. Well, if you're so blended how come I've never seen you dance like a black woman?

HARRIET. Well I've not had the call for it.

BEN. You've not had the call for it?

HARRIET. Yes.

BEN. Why, is it some special signal that only certain people can hear?

HARRIET. I've never wanted to stick out.

SARAH. What about now?

HARRIET. What do you – [mean]?

SARAH *puts some music on from her phone – It's 'Crazy in Love' by Beyoncé ft. Jay-Z.*

I can't dance now!

SARAH. Well, that doesn't sound very black. They dance everywhere. Come on, Harriet. Let's see your black woman come out.

BEN. Okay –

SARAH. Your inner black woman.

JAMES. Go on.

SARAH. Let's see it.

BEN. Harriet –

HARRIET. Stop it! I'm sorry he's –

SARAH. Go on!

HARRIET. All right. Okay. Okay.

> HARRIET *starts to dance. It's not very good.* SARAH *and* JAMES *try not to laugh.*

BEN. Okay, stop. Stop. That's enough! You've had your fun.

HARRIET. Well of course, I've lost it a bit.

SARAH. It's really good.

BEN. Harriet –

HARRIET. Well, I used to get a lot of attention with it.

BEN. I said come on.

HARRIET. I don't know why you're being so – When they're being so kind and understanding.

BEN. Understanding? They know, Harriet. It's a joke. This is a joke.

HARRIET. Don't be so –

BEN. Harriet –

HARRIET. They wouldn't joke about this. No one would joke about this.

BEN. Harriet, if you saw a person dancing like that, you'd think they were mad not black.

HARRIET. Now you're being offensive. Racist.

BEN. I'm being racist? To who?

HARRIET. To me.

BEN. For fuckssake, Harriet, they know it was you who called the police!

Silence.

Look, mate, I don't blame you for being pissed. If it was me, if it was me, I would feel the same. Cos what they did to you was bang out of order. Doing that in front of your kid. They wouldn't have done that to a white person. They would've approached him. Asked questions first. They wouldn't wrestle them to the ground. You can't feel white because being white is how you're treated!

Silence.

SARAH (*knowingly*). *You* called them?

HARRIET (*anxious*). Ben?

BEN. She's been digging at us constantly.

SARAH. I'm sorry?

BEN. And then there's the lies. The lies about the boxing.

A pause.

HARRIET. But we apologised. It's fine.

SARAH. When did you apologise?

HARRIET. When we spoke about misunderstandings. I thought –

SARAH. Misunderstandings? An apology is actually saying the words, 'I'm sorry'. Asking how someone is. Asking how my daughter is. Not saying how happy you are for her that she's not addicted to crack.

BEN. All right. Calm down.

SARAH. Please don't tell me to calm down.

JAMES. Sarah, I think we should all calm down.

BEN. My wife made a mistake, which you said, yourself, anyone would make.

SARAH. So that means we don't get a proper apology? My family deserves an apology.

BEN. She tried to.

SARAH. Our child has night terrors now, coincidentally.

BEN. I mean, she came here in good faith –

SARAH. She's / four.

BEN. She doesn't deserve this! To be treated like this!

SARAH. *She* doesn't deserve?

BEN. She's bent over backward to be kind but from the start you've been really aggressive.

JAMES. Now, come on.

BEN. Aggressive and intimidating.

SARAH. I'm aggressive and intimidating?

BEN. Yes.

JAMES. She called the police!

HARRIET. The girl was screaming! She was screaming I want my mum! I want my mum! She was screaming, the girl, your girl. And I was afraid. Afraid to go up to you in case I made things worse and afraid to not do something so I did something. I called them. Yeah, maybe I should've gone up to you but you're a man and I didn't know what you looked like or what Victoria looked like because you're not a friend on Facebook and Louisa never said. You should've friended us on Facebook. I try to do the right thing but, somehow, it's always wrong.

A pause.

Maybe we should – We were only meant to be here for five minutes. It's late and we've left the boys for too long as it is. They're probably running riot as we speak. Burning the house down. Not that I've left them home alone. I would never do that.

In silence, JAMES *and* SARAH *escort* BEN *and* HARRIET *towards the door.*

The tea's been lovely.

SARAH. Thank you.

JAMES. Thanks again for the muffins.

HARRIET. Not a problem.

JAMES. And the cake.

HARRIET. Thank you.

SARAH. When do you want the basket back?

HARRIET. Keep it. It's not expensive. Or bring it back whenever –

JAMES. Right.

HARRIET. Great. And if you could let us know about the pub quiz. The team, you know, could do with the support.

HARRIET and BEN exit.

A long silence.

SARAH. Is it me?

JAMES. You did nothing wrong.

SARAH. Then why –

JAMES. Sarah –

SARAH. – do I feel like I'm the bad person?

JAMES. You did nothing wrong. They seemed apologetic at the beginning, anyway.

A pause.

SARAH. I'd better clear up.

JAMES. I'll finish down here.

SARAH. No, you need to rest.

JAMES. I'm fine. Really.

JAMES takes plates out into the kitchen. SARAH just stands there for a few moments then, during the following conversation, she slowly takes off her clothes, folds them and puts them on the sofa. She then takes off her wig and puts it on top of the pile.

(*Off.*) She seemed to be really interested in the Bonetta story. That Harriet?

SARAH. She was probably just being polite. The only thing she seemed interested in was her lemon drizzle cake.

JAMES (*off*). That was weird, wasn't it?

SARAH. Completely obsessed. Not too much lemon rind?

JAMES *laughs*.

He was aggressive.

JAMES (*off*). He *was* aggressive, wasn't he?

SARAH. Maybe it's a northern thing.

JAMES *laughs, off*.

Silence.

JAMES (*off*). You don't think I'm missing a trick not writing about Bonetta and focusing solely on Alice, do you? I know they weren't the most pleasant of people but they might be on to something.

SARAH. I really don't think people will be that interested. What did she actually do?

JAMES (*off*). The story could delve into their friendship.

SARAH. The money's in royalty and sex.

JAMES (*off*). I suppose I could write an essay on her. Submit it to one of the journals. I need to update my publishing record. It could be about Queen Victoria's role as benefactor. Something like that.

JAMES *gets a text*.

I've just got a text from somebody called Leon. He's holding a spoken-word night next month and wants to present something about my experience with the police. What should I say? I don't even know who he is.

Naked, SARAH *walks out of the house*.

He's definitely not one of mine. But they've probably been talking about it. Black boys keep coming up to me in the corridors and fist bumping me.

JAMES *comes out of the kitchen and sees* SARAH*'s abandoned clothes and wig. He picks them up, thinking she's gone upstairs. He follows up.*

I mean, I do feel angry about it when I think about it, but I suppose the thing to do is not to think about it.

ACT THREE

Windsor Castle, 1867

The opulence of a royal residence.

SARAH *and* SARAH BONETTA *are seated. They are partway through having tea.* SARAH *is dressed for a day at the office. A spear rests against the table. There is a small bust of Prince Albert somewhere in the room.*

QUEEN VICTORIA *is under a table, head first.* QUEEN VICTORIA *can neither see nor hear* SARAH. *She speaks to Victoria,* SARAH BONETTA*'s four-year-old daughter, who is also under the table. We do not ever see the child, although we may hear her.*

QUEEN VICTORIA. Would you like a chocolate nib?

A pause.

Would you like a chocolate nib? They're jolly good.

SARAH BONETTA. Victoria, come out of there, please?

A pause.

QUEEN VICTORIA. She's a shy little thing, isn't she? Victoria? Or shall I call you Vicky? Does she like to be called Vicky?

SARAH BONETTA. I don't think / she [does] –

QUEEN VICTORIA. I shall call her Little Vicky. Would you like a chocolate nib, Little Vicky?

SARAH BONETTA. She won't answer to it.

QUEEN VICTORIA. Little Vicky?

QUEEN VICTORIA *eventually comes up.*

You were saying. What were you saying? Yes. The school…

QUEEN VICTORIA *sits and sips her tea. The two* SARAHS *lift their cups and sip.*

SARAH BONETTA. Yes, Ma'am. I was saying that I've been teaching them several subjects among which are economics, physics and German –

QUEEN VICTORIA. Yes, well, everyone needs to speak German.

SARAH BONETTA. And etiquette, of course.

QUEEN VICTORIA. How have they taken to etiquette?

SARAH BONETTA. Quite spectacularly. Whenever the British Emissaries visit and have tea, they say it's impossible to distinguish between host and guest. Ma'am, my school has become the most sought-after institution for girls to attend throughout the entire protectorate. It has a waiting list of twelve months.

QUEEN VICTORIA. Well, that's as I expected. And to think the naysayers said it would be impossible to bring the natives up beyond the level of darning and needlework. Jolly good.

SARAH BONETTA *glances at* SARAH, *who discreetly signals for her to get on with it.*

SARAH BONETTA. Of course it isn't all plain sailing.

QUEEN VICTORIA. Nothing of importance ever is.

SARAH BONETTA. Yes, I suppose. There are some girls who just won't cooperate. They refuse to take on a Christian name and keep little figurines of their gods in their desks.

QUEEN VICTORIA. Habits you beat out of them, I hope.

SARAH BONETTA. Some of them abscond because of it. There was one particular child who –

QUEEN VICTORIA. Is this going to take long?

SARAH BONETTA. Well, no. Not really. I just thought you'd like to hear / about –

QUEEN VICTORIA. We succeeded, Sally. That's all that counts. Not the casualties.

SARAH BONETTA. Yes, Ma'am. But I wouldn't call them casualties.

QUEEN VICTORIA. What else would you call them?

Silence.

SARAH BONETTA. Let me tell you about this child. This child, Ma'am, she was quite spectacular. She believed one of their gods spoke to her through candlelight. It made me think how similar their beliefs are to ours. They have a girl who claims to have communion with one of their gods through a candlewick and we have Moses conversing with God via a burning bush.

QUEEN VICTORIA. She rather reminds me of myself. I used to hide under the tables when I was her size. Particularly when my uncle had an audience. Although I was eight not four. I could fit under anything if I rightly recall up until the age of twelve. Scurrying along the secret passages listening in to conversations. There are passages behind these walls, you know. In case we are ever besieged. But no one could fit inside them except me. And the grandchildren, of course, when they're playing hide-and-seek. Perhaps she would like a dolly. (*To Victoria.*) Would you rather have a dolly?

QUEEN VICTORIA *goes to her bureau.*

SARAH. I'm so sorry.

SARAH BONETTA. Please. Don't speak.

SARAH. She's isn't going to –

SARAH BONETTA. I'm not listening.

SARAH. She isn't going to –

SARAH BONETTA (*covers her ears*). Fa-la-la-tring.

SARAH. I'm on your side, Aina. Really.

QUEEN VICTORIA. Sally?

SARAH BONETTA. Yes, Ma'am?

QUEEN VICTORIA. Will she take to a dolly?

SARAH BONETTA. Usually.

QUEEN VICTORIA. All girls love dolls. They're such pretty little things.

SARAH BONETTA. Victoria *do* come out. It was just a silly little spear. The Queen was simply showing me how to use it.

QUEEN VICTORIA. I wasn't even aggressive with it. Don't worry. I'll get her out. I'm quite used to a fragile child.

QUEEN VICTORIA *approaches with a little doll.*

I had names for every one of them as a girl. I believe this one is Sophie.

QUEEN VICTORIA *speaks to Victoria as she waves the doll under the table.*

Little Vicky? Would you like a friend? This is Sophie. Isn't she pretty?

There is a giggle from under the table. Victoria takes the doll.

We have made a connection! I knew we would.

Victoria throws the doll back.

SARAH BONETTA. Victoria!

QUEEN VICTORIA. She's quite a feral little thing, isn't she?

QUEEN VICTORIA *sits down. Only when* QUEEN VICTORIA *eats do the two* SARAHS *eat. This is the etiquette.* QUEEN VICTORIA *is a messy eater.* QUEEN VICTORIA *sips her tea. The two* SARAHS *lift their cups and sip.*

Children bring such joy.

SARAH BONETTA. They really do, Ma'am. I have never felt such love for any being until I had Victoria.

QUEEN VICTORIA. Husband excepting, of course.

SARAH BONETTA. Yes, of course. As you know, I didn't think James and I were suited when we first met but things changed drastically when we were in Africa.

QUEEN VICTORIA. I was wondering when I'd get my dues.

SARAH. Tick-tock. Tick-tock.

SARAH BONETTA. Thank you for introducing us, Ma'am. He suits me perfectly.

QUEEN VICTORIA. Yes, well I always got top marks for that sort of thing.

SARAH BONETTA. The passion he had to better / the natives.

QUEEN VICTORIA. In some ways he reminds me of my
Albert. That bullishness. Just remember to always keep his
interest. Albie and I used to play at living in a small cottage
in Shropshire. He would pretend to be a milkherd and
I a milkherd's wife. He always wanted to make cheeses.
(*Re: bust.*) It's a perfect likeness, isn't it?

SARAH BONETTA. Yes, Ma'am.

QUEEN VICTORIA *is momentarily lost in her reverie.*
Then:

QUEEN VICTORIA. You helped pave the way for a future of
English African women, Sally. Jolly good.

SARAH BONETTA. It's just a shame their suitors don't think so.

QUEEN VICTORIA. Sorry?

SARAH BONETTA. Their suitors. They won't take to toad in
the hole. Or having tea at four o'clock. It's actually getting to
be such a chore that the girls now want to come here to
secure a marriage.

QUEEN VICTORIA. Marriage to whom?

SARAH BONETTA. Well, to the English.

QUEEN VICTORIA. No. No. They're meant to be English over
there not over here.

SARAH BONETTA. I didn't think it mattered.

QUEEN VICTORIA. Of course it matters. We're *expanding* the
Empire. There's no point them coming back here, is there?

SARAH. You see? What more proof do you need?

QUEEN VICTORIA. You must teach the native men how to eat
toad in the hole. There's absolutely nothing wrong with it.

SARAH. Look, I get it. You have feelings... Attachment.

SARAH BONETTA. Stop it.

SARAH. Oh my God! You actually love her!

SARAH BONETTA. She's my mother, of course I love her!
She raised me. She saved me.

SARAH. Even though deep down you feel –

SARAH BONETTA. You have no idea how I feel.

SARAH. And she didn't raise you. There was Mrs Schoen and Mrs Forbes. Even Mrs Phipps had a hand in it.

SARAH BONETTA. Whatever. My life was spectacular. Is spectacular.

SARAH. Really?

> QUEEN VICTORIA *gets up. The two* SARAHS *put down their teacups.*

QUEEN VICTORIA. We shall be courageous and move the table.

SARAH BONETTA. Yes, Ma'am.

> QUEEN VICTORIA *and* SARAH BONETTA *get up and approach the table.*

SARAH. If it's any consolation, I did think about someone else / but –

SARAH BONETTA. Who?

> *Silence.*

> Who?

SARAH. Lord Lugard if you must know.

QUEEN VICTORIA. You go there, Sally, and I'll stay here.

SARAH BONETTA. Who?

SARAH. Lugard. Lugard claims that he created Nigeria.

SARAH BONETTA. I haven't a clue what you're talking about.

SARAH. It's what he names the northern and southern protectorates in 1914. He also claims that his system of indirect rule was a success. It wasn't.

SARAH BONETTA. Again, I don't –

QUEEN VICTORIA. After three.

SARAH. The British created – (*Air quotes.*) 'tribal' leaders to impose British rule on their own people.

QUEEN VICTORIA. One, two, three.

They try to move the table.

SARAH. I mean, how could a system that held a gun to the head of a people who had their own form of governance be expected to work?

QUEEN VICTORIA. Come on, Sally! Put some welly into it!

SARAH. When you push people down they will eventually push back and it's not necessarily with violence. In Nigeria's case it's with corruption. Obviously.

SARAH BONETTA *begins coughing.*

Are you all right?

QUEEN VICTORIA. Sally?

SARAH BONETTA. I'm all right, Ma'am. Really.

QUEEN VICTORIA. Bosh! Sit.

QUEEN VICTORIA *fetches* SARAH BONETTA *a glass of water.* SARAH BONETTA *sits.*

SARAH BONETTA. I'm sorry.

SARAH. And then there's China. It's there now. Plundering Nigeria under the guise of offering help and solutions, just like she did.

SARAH BONETTA. Oh, do stop going on. Please!

SARAH. Don't you see? Nigeria would be great if it hadn't been for her. It has all this oil. It's one of the richest countries in the world yet has one of the highest levels of poverty. It's because of / the –

SARAH BONETTA. Because of the corruption. Yes. Yes. I get it.

QUEEN VICTORIA. We clearly need another pair of hands.

QUEEN VICTORIA *pulls the cord for the servant's bell.*

SARAH. There's a famous Nigerian saying: The fish rots from the head. With Lugard we just don't go back far enough. Sorry.

Silence.

QUEEN VICTORIA. Better?

SARAH BONETTA *nods*.

Silence.

They'll take an age to send someone, you know. Yesterday it took half an hour. Albie used to look after all of that. (*To bust*.) Didn't you, dear? Nowadays it's all a bit of a hotchpotch. I sacked the ones I didn't trust. They all think I'm off my trolley, Sally. Mad with grief. Think I've got what grandfather had. You think I don't know what they say about me beyond these walls? How they want to do away with me?

SARAH BONETTA. That's not true, Ma'am.

QUEEN VICTORIA. You're really quite sweet.

QUEEN VICTORIA *has another chocolate nib*.

Cocoa. James can't go wrong with cocoa. I wasn't particularly keen on the palm-oil farm. I wasn't at all surprised to hear that the project collapsed.

SARAH BONETTA. It collapsed only because the investors reneged on the contracts. James was always quite the gentleman but it didn't seem to matter.

QUEEN VICTORIA. Oh I see.

SARAH BONETTA. You do? Really?

QUEEN VICTORIA. Yes, of course I do.

SARAH BONETTA. Oh, Ma'am, I'm so relieved! They behaved quite unreasonably towards him. Over there, they're all adamant they want to progress the Society's mission of abandonment and treat us equally, but instead they behave in a way that's quite the opposite. I think they're quite unchristian.

QUEEN VICTORIA. Well, the good news is that no one is producing chocolate in Lagos. So he'll have a monopoly.

SARAH BONETTA. But it's not James's fault that the farm collapsed, / Ma'am.

QUEEN VICTORIA. It will be impossible for him to fail.

Silence.

SARAH BONETTA. I thought you said you understood?

QUEEN VICTORIA. Of course I understand and it pleases me to see such ardent support of your husband, but you mustn't distress yourself.

SARAH BONETTA. Ma'am –

QUEEN VICTORIA. A woman with a commercial head causes too much ill-ease in a marriage. I know. I had to back down on several occasions myself but he did compensate me in other areas.

A beat.

The making of children numbers four, five and six.

SARAH BONETTA. Do you think Africans can be more, Ma'am?

QUEEN VICTORIA. More than what?

SARAH BONETTA. More than what you say we can be.

QUEEN VICTORIA. One can only be what one is capable of being. No more. No less.

SARAH BONETTA *coughs.*

I really thought your constitution might have improved with all that heat. Have you been taking your tincture?

SARAH BONETTA. Of course I have and I've told you all it doesn't work. I've told you all a hundred times. The heat doesn't work. My cough isn't due to the weather otherwise every African living in England would have one as well.

Silence.

I'm sorry.

Silence.

I went to a witch doctor. Yes, I know it's taboo but people swore by him. White people, too. So I went out of curiosity. I took what he offered and I felt better for it. He didn't cure me but neither has Dr Jenner.

QUEEN VICTORIA. What is it they call it?

SARAH BONETTA. What?

QUEEN VICTORIA. That condition.

SARAH. Aina, it's time.

QUEEN VICTORIA. That phrase.

SARAH. You've seen how she is.

QUEEN VICTORIA. It's on the tip of my tongue.

SARAH. You can't tell her she's wrong.

QUEEN VICTORIA. Gone native. That's what they say, isn't it?

SARAH BONETTA. I haven't gone native.

SARAH. She'll only take offence and will punish you later for it.

QUEEN VICTORIA. Then what's all this gibberish?

SARAH. Colonialism doesn't work, Aina. And it's not just in Africa.

SARAH BONETTA. Ma'am, it's important that you see –

SARAH. It doesn't work over here.

QUEEN VICTORIA. Would one even know if one had turned native, Sally? I hear it occurs insidiously.

SARAH. You see, we keep coming and coming, we, the African English, but we're not wanted like she says. So we're crushed and killed and incarcerated.

SARAH BONETTA. I apologise, Ma'am. I didn't realise I'd changed so drastically. I thought I was being my usual self.

SARAH. Her tyranny exists in many forms, Aina.

QUEEN VICTORIA. You are. Of sorts.

SARAH. Forms that push us down. Lessen us. Forms designed to make them feel superior.

QUEEN VICTORIA. Sally, our past meetings were fun.

SARAH. Oh yes, they'll never say it.

QUEEN VICTORIA. All that intellectual back-and-forth.

SARAH. Never use the word. Not the worst ones, anyway.

QUEEN VICTORIA. But you're a woman now. Married.

SARAH. She's doing it now.

QUEEN VICTORIA. You have other priorities.

SARAH. Pushing you down.

QUEEN VICTORIA. Your husband needs you by his side. Especially now, with his new venture.

SARAH. The bins bulge at the seams with us, Aina.

SARAH BONETTA. The bins?

SARAH. Loony. Bulging from all their tripping-ups and misunderstandings and belittlings and lying and underestimatings and distrustings and underminings and shrinkings.

QUEEN VICTORIA. And you're to give up the school.

SARAH BONETTA. But I enjoy the school.

QUEEN VICTORIA. Sally, I know what's best for you.

SARAH. They seem like tiny things, Aina. These things they do to us. These assaults. But they're cumulative. Piling on top of each other, pushing us down, overwhelming us until the madness sets in.

Silence.

SARAH BONETTA. I'm sorry. You're right. I am confused. There is so much heat out there. It's a different type of heat.

SARAH. A different type of heat?

SARAH BONETTA (*to* SARAH). Yes! (*To* QUEEN VICTORIA.) Makes one quite giddy. Takes time to adjust. One forgets sometimes how to be.

QUEEN VICTORIA. You are quite right, Sally.

SARAH BONETTA. Will you show me again how to use the spear, Ma'am? We never finished what we were doing.

QUEEN VICTORIA. Oh yes. The spear. Yes. We didn't quite finish with it, did we? I suppose now that the child is out of the way we have our freedom.

QUEEN VICTORIA *picks up the spear and demonstrates.*

It's such a splendid gift, Sally. Thank you. But as I was telling you, the Yoruba Chief who gave you this has got it all wrong.

SARAH. They're still frightened, you see. Frightened that we'll attack them or eat them even.

SARAH BONETTA. What?

QUEEN VICTORIA. I said the Chief is quite wrong.

SARAH. Or they think that we're better than them.

QUEEN VICTORIA. This is how Albie showed me how it works.

SARAH. Or it's just we're too different. An aberration.

QUEEN VICTORIA. He was a dab hand at weaponry.

SARAH. Who knows? But fear's why they do it.

QUEEN VICTORIA. You use your left hand to aim. Now, come at me.

SARAH. Assault us constantly.

SARAH BONETTA. I don't have a weapon.

SARAH. Yes. Always one rule for them and one rule for you.

QUEEN VICTORIA *bobs about* SARAH BONETTA, *threating her with the spear.*

QUEEN VICTORIA. Do your worst, Sally.

SARAH. Eroding. Lessening. An uneven playing field.

QUEEN VICTORIA *runs at* SARAH BONETTA *with the spear. She lets out a roar.*

SARAH BONETTA. Ma'am!

QUEEN VICTORIA *collapses into her chair, still holding the spear, breathless.*

QUEEN VICTORIA. We do have such fun, don't we?

Silence.

Such a funny little thing, isn't it? To think after all their years of existence, this is all they could come up with.

SARAH. Come on, Aina! Aren't you sick of this?

SARAH BONETTA. It's fine.

SARAH. It's not.

SARAH BONETTA. It is. It is. It is.

SARAH. I know you feel it.

SARAH BONETTA. I don't.

SARAH. Have felt it, then.

    SARAH BONETTA *gets up and pushes the table.*

QUEEN VICTORIA. Sally, what on earth are you doing?

SARAH BONETTA (*to* QUEEN VICTORIA). I'm trying again, Ma'am.

QUEEN VICTORIA. Don't be silly. We shall have help.

SARAH BONETTA. I've indulged Victoria enough, Ma'am. Really.

    QUEEN VICTORIA *rings the bell again.*

SARAH. It starts in schools with the undermarking. At work with the underpaying. Last to be interviewed. Last in the queue. And you can't put your finger on one thing because it's everywhere. Stemming from a belief that we're not as good. It's quite clever, really.

SARAH BONETTA. Why can't you just ignore it? Madness just for that?

SARAH. People have gone mad for less.

QUEEN VICTORIA. Didn't I tell you? They do it on purpose. To punish me.

    QUEEN VICTORIA *rings the bell again.*

SARAH BONETTA. How do you know all of this?

SARAH. A while back I had an epiphany. I saw how the world is. They wouldn't listen, so I found you.

SARAH BONETTA. But why me?

SARAH. Because we must be united in this. All of us.

QUEEN VICTORIA. He's behind it. The eldest.

SARAH BONETTA. But they can't be all bad. There are good people. Kind people.

SARAH. Yes. There are some good people. But even good people assault us subconsciously.

SARAH BONETTA. I don't believe you.

QUEEN VICTORIA. You don't believe that the Palace is punishing me? Sally, I might be the ruler of the British Empire. Invincible. But here, in the Palace, you really can't trust family.

SARAH. You see, each individual acts separately but together these assaults create a glass ceiling that permeates all sections of society. It's safety in numbers, basically.

SARAH BONETTA. Sorry.

QUEEN VICTORIA. It's not your fault.

SARAH. And when you complain they don't want to talk about it.

QUEEN VICTORIA. You think the eldest will be able to parent the colonies? Bosh!

SARAH. Say we're whining, whinging, criticising.

QUEEN VICTORIA. Still, I've survived numerous attempts on my life. I'm impossible to assassinate, evidently.

SARAH. I don't hate them, if that's what you think. They can't understand what they never experience. Oppression. Are you listening?

SARAH BONETTA (*to* QUEEN VICTORIA). I'm going to go again, Ma'am.

QUEEN VICTORIA. I said to wait, Sally.

SARAH. Aina, people will never give up on a system which benefits them willingly.

SARAH BONETTA. After three.

SARAH. So we must stop begging.

QUEEN VICTORIA. Sally?

SARAH BONETTA. One, two –

SARAH. Do we not deserve to be powerful? Do we not deserve success?

SARAH BONETTA. Three!

SARAH BONETTA *moves the table all by herself.*

QUEEN VICTORIA. Sally!

SARAH. What makes them more important?

SARAH BONETTA *looks under the table.*

SARAH BONETTA. Victoria… Victoria! (*Suddenly panicked.*) Where is she?

QUEEN VICTORIA. What?

SARAH. In many years you will be written about in their history.

SARAH BONETTA. She's not there. Victoria! (*To* SARAH.) What have you done with her?

SARAH. Not much, a few pages.

SARAH BONETTA. Answer me!

QUEEN VICTORIA. She must have discovered the walls. Such a clever little thing. Quickly!

SARAH. A children's book, perhaps. You will barely be called by your birth name.

QUEEN VICTORIA *and* SARAH BONETTA *pull back the table further. There is an opening in the wall.*

QUEEN VICTORIA. She can't have gone far.

SARAH. You are someone who your Queen rescued from a certain death by a savage.

QUEEN VICTORIA *listens to the walls.*

You will be seen as a portrait of her benevolence.

QUEEN VICTORIA. Can you hear her?

SARAH BONETTA *listens against the wall.*

SARAH. Throughout history we are viewed as a people who cannot save ourselves. Who do not exist without the whites.

QUEEN VICTORIA. Sally?

SARAH. But it's not true. We exist. Before her, you see, we were kings and queens, scientists, merchants, traders, travellers, deep-sea divers. Yes! Divers. Famous divers. We swim. Our women were objects of admiration, adoration, veneration. Written about in poetry. We were everything before her. Before the lies about our inferiority set in. Before we were written out of history.

SARAH BONETTA. Victoria, please!

QUEEN VICTORIA. Sally?

SARAH. Let us have our history, but not with her as our saviour but you. Kill the Queen. Go down in our history as the one who gave us our freedom.

Silence.

QUEEN VICTORIA. Sally, Africa has most certainly changed you, despite your protests.

SARAH BONETTA. Maybe it has. I don't know.

Silence.

QUEEN VICTORIA. Funchal.

SARAH BONETTA. Sorry?

QUEEN VICTORIA. Funchal. I shall tell James to send you there to rest.

SARAH BONETTA. But I'm resting in Africa.

QUEEN VICTORIA. You said it yourself. It's a different type of heat. I have lodgings. You'll have a wonderful view of the sea. He won't be able to look after the child on his own, of course, so she'll stay here with me.

SARAH BONETTA. With you?

QUEEN VICTORIA. Yes. She's my godchild, after all.

SARAH BONETTA. But I can't – I don't want to – [leave her] –

QUEEN VICTORIA. Or she can stay with the Schoens or the Phipps or whoever and come and visit. She'll have a marvellous time just like you did.

SARAH BONETTA. I was miserable!

A beat.

I'm sorry. Ma'am, I appreciate that I had a better life and I am grateful and thankful and I know you all loved me but –

SARAH. Say it.

SARAH BONETTA. It's just she's so young.

QUEEN VICTORIA. Bosh! You were the same age when you came to me.

SARAH BONETTA. I was seven. She's four.

SARAH. Say it…

SARAH BONETTA. She needs…

SARAH. You didn't ever feel comfortable.

SARAH BONETTA. She needs…

SARAH. You didn't ever feel beautiful.

QUEEN VICTORIA. I know what she needs, Sally.

SARAH. You were cleverer than the lot of them.

SARAH BONETTA. Stop.

QUEEN VICTORIA. I know what's best for you.

SARAH. She's the worst.

QUEEN VICTORIA. Come.

QUEEN VICTORIA *opens out her arms to* SARAH BONETTA *benevolently.*

SARAH. Writing such terrible things about you. In her diary. How terrifyingly black you looked.

SARAH BONETTA *hesitates.*

Why would I lie to you? Your own mother, who you believe loves you.

SARAH BONETTA *grabs the spear, threatens* SARAH.

SARAH BONETTA. I said stop. Stop!

SARAH. She doesn't love you, Aina. How can she? She can't love what she fears. What person can? The most they can ever do is try to contain it.

SARAH BONETTA *is incredibly distressed*.

QUEEN VICTORIA. She's moving! Quick! Sally! Sally! This turret leads to the Blue drawing room. Stay here in case she comes back on herself. I shall race to the Blue drawing room. Little Vicky! I'm coming to get you! What shall we do with naughty little African girls when we catch you? We shall gobble you up, that's what. We shall gobble you up. We shall gobble you up until you are good.

SARAH BONETTA *lunges at* QUEEN VICTORIA *with the spear and stabs her with it. She drops the spear, immediately.*

SARAH BONETTA (*horrified*). I'm sorry, Ma'am! I really don't know what came over me. She said… She said…

Silence.

(*To* SARAH.) Help her.

SARAH *remains where she is*.

Mother…

SARAH BONETTA *falls to the ground sobs, cradles, comforts the dying* QUEEN.

Her sobbing lasts for a few moments as QUEEN VICTORIA *dies.*

Where's my daughter?

SARAH. She's in the Blue drawing room. Just like she said.

Silence.

SARAH BONETTA. What's going to happen now?

SARAH. I don't know.

SARAH BONETTA. What?

SARAH. It's okay. Don't be scared. Because from all that I've seen… all that I've seen, Aina, what's going to happen from this day on will be better than what has gone before. So trust what you've done is good. Will you trust in us, Aina? Will you trust?

SARAH *holds out her hand.* SARAH BONETTA *takes hold of it.*

I will.

End.

Addendum

Telephone conversation for Sarah in Act Two

SARAH. Of course. Of course. Of course. It's exactly what I've been wanting to sink my teeth into.

ANDY HEAD. That's what I thought when I chose you for the project. I thought this is one for Sarah. You're excited, yes?...

SARAH. I'm excited. I'm incredibly excited...

ANDY HEAD. That's what I like to hear.

SARAH. I am so excited. Really. You really need to see my face to see just how excited I am.

ANDY HEAD. I said to the team, Sarah knows the country. Sarah's been there before.

SARAH. No, I have never been before –

ANDY HEAD. But you're from Africa...

SARAH. I am...

ANDY HEAD. Nigeria, right?

SARAH. That's right. Originally. Yes. My parents were born there...

ANDY HEAD. And you've never been?

SARAH. Well, I haven't had any real desire to go.

ANDY HEAD. Really?

SARAH. Really. I thought I mentioned that before, Andy. Several times. There are just so many other countries that I prefer. Like Hong Kong, Malaysia. The whole of Southeast Asia. But I'm excited to be going now. Incredibly excited. Although I thought Rich Webb would have been your first choice...

ANDY HEAD. Well, Rich isn't quite the / right fit.

SARAH. But I'm excited. God I'm excited. All that culture...

ANDY HEAD. All that culture will be an experience for you if you've never been, won't it?

SARAH. Yes, it will be an experience. I had a feeling that's what you were going to say.

ANDY HEAD. So it's pretty much a win-win. Look, I'm about to be cut off. Reception's poor.

SARAH. Okay. Great.

ANDY HEAD. Maria has the details of the offer.

SARAH. Great. I'll talk to Maria on Monday...

ANDY HEAD. Have a good weekend.

SARAH. You too. Thanks, Andy, have a great weekend.

A Nick Hern Book

The Gift first published in Great Britain in 2020 as a paperback original by Nick Hern Books Limited, The Glasshouse, 49a Goldhawk Road, London W12 8QP, in association with Eclipse Theatre and Belgrade Theatre Coventry

The Gift copyright © 2020 Janice Okoh

Janice Okoh has asserted her moral right to be identified as the author of this work

Cover artwork by AKA

Designed and typeset by Nick Hern Books, London
Printed in the UK by Mimeo Ltd, Huntingdon, Cambridgeshire PE29 6XX

A CIP catalogue record for this book is available from the British Library

ISBN 978 1 84842 947 5

www.nickhernbooks.co.uk

facebook.com/nickhernbooks

twitter.com/nickhernbooks